# Recipes for Adventure II

## The Best of Trail Bytes

Adventures in Dehydrating Backpacking Food

Published by
Backpacking Chef Publishing
PO Box 482
Waleska, GA 30183
www.BackpackingChef.com



ISBN: 978-1-7374630-0-9

*To Vögelchen, the "little bird" with whom I share the trail of life and love.*
*Thank you for your abounding love and support, and for taste-testing all my experiments.*

***Special Thanks:***
Interior Design by Jamie Tipton, Open Heart Designs, www.openheartdesigns.com
Editing by Lindsey Nelson, Exact Edits, www.exactedits.com.

# Contents

## 6. POTATO RECIPES 70



## 7. BARLEY RECIPES 76



## 8. MACARONI & TOMATO SAUCE 82



## 9. COLD-SOAK SALADS 88

# Introduction

## What's New in Recipes for Adventure II

In my monthly newsletter, *Trail Bytes*, I write about dehydrating food for the trail. Each issue features a backpacking recipe and a food-drying project. After 100 issues, a collection of that work is presented here in *Recipes for Adventure II: The Best of Trail Bytes*.

Now that BackpackingChef.com and *Trail Bytes* are viewed by an international audience, the book has metric equivalents for weight, volume, and temperature. You'll still see the usual cups and tablespoons, but now you can also see measurements in grams and milliliters and temperatures in Fahrenheit and Celsius.

Cooking directions show how to rehydrate meals in a thermos food jar as well as in a pot. Thermos cooking lets you prepare dehydrated meals in advance—for work, travel, and trail. Meals rehydrate better with longer soak times. A thermos holds its temperature for hours, whether you're rehydrating a stew with boiled water or a macaroni, quinoa, or couscous salad with cold water.

Chapter One wakes up the breakfast category with Omelet Bites, Overnight Muesli, Tortilla Grits Bowls, and Pancake Bites. For something hot and creamy, try the Cream of Pancakes topped with pecan pieces. Omelet Bites incorporate grated potatoes, which ensures that the eggs will rehydrate well.

Chapter Two features the all-new soup category, including techniques for turning dehydrated meals into soup. It's a good practice to use up dehydrated food when the hiking season is over; making soup is an easy way to do it. The chapter has several delicious soup recipes, including a super-healthy vegetable-soup powder that can be used as the base for creating unlimited soups by adding dehydrated meat, tofu, vegetables, starches, or beans. A hearty fish chowder recipe rounds out the collection.

Chapter Three covers how to dehydrate tofu. With one simple step, the problem of tofu not rehydrating well is solved.

Tofu absorbs flavors well, which carry over to dehydrated meals. Learn how to precook tofu with vegetable, curry, and taco seasonings. You don't have to be vegetarian to enjoy Spicy-Tofu Tortillas, Tofu Noodles with Vegetables & Rice, and Curry Tofu & Vegetables.

Chapter Four shows how to dehydrate beans, lentils, and quinoa. Recipes include 3 Sisters Stew, Green-Lentil Chili, Inca Stew, Red-Lentil Curry, Green Lentil Stew, and Zucchini Ratatouille. Since sweet potatoes go well with these meals, there are also instructions for dehydrating baked sweet potatoes.

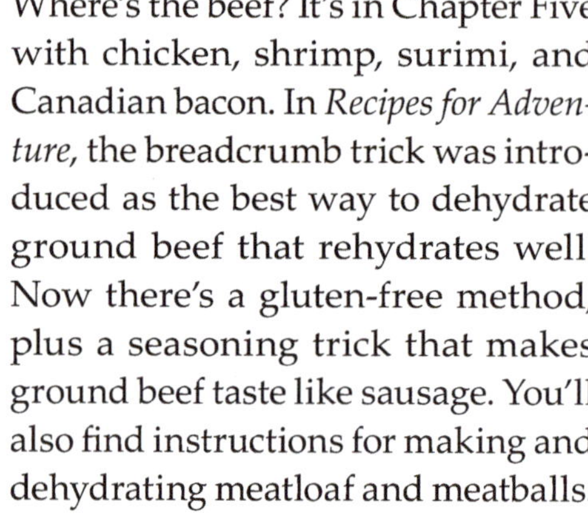

Where's the beef? It's in Chapter Five with chicken, shrimp, surimi, and Canadian bacon. In *Recipes for Adventure*, the breadcrumb trick was introduced as the best way to dehydrate ground beef that rehydrates well. Now there's a gluten-free method, plus a seasoning trick that makes ground beef taste like sausage. You'll also find instructions for making and dehydrating meatloaf and meatballs.

Dried chicken has always been *tough* to rehydrate. Dehydrating canned chicken is one solution, but new methods are presented for drying pressure-cooked chicken and drying ground chicken and turkey.

Chapter Six focuses on potatoes. Potato bark can take a bit of spirited stirring to rehydrate back into mashed potatoes. It also has a reputation for puncturing vacuum-sealed bags. Learn how to turn potato bark into potato powder that rehydrates almost instantly. For more texture in meals, try dehydrating grated potatoes. Recipes include Grated Potatoes with Sauerkraut and Ham, Grated Potatoes with Vegetables and Beef, and Grated Potatoes & Chili.

Chapter Seven explores cooking and dehydrating barley. Meals with barley are a nice change from rice. Recipes include Barley Risotto and Beef & Barley with Fennel, plus how to turn these meals into soups.

Chapter Eight shows how to dry macaroni and homemade tomato sauce. The sauce is ground into tomato-sauce powder. The chapter includes instructions for dehydrating Italian-seasoned San Marzano tomatoes and olives. Those items are used in meals like Beefy Macaroni & Tomato Sauce, as well as in cold-soak salads.

Looking for no-cook backpacking meals? Chapter Nine covers cold-soak salad recipes, including Tuna & Macaroni San Marzano, Couscous Salad with Cucumber-Salsa Dressing, Quinoa & Bean Cilantro Salad, Shrimp Cocktail Tortillas, Sushi Rice Bowl Salad, and Peach Salsa Rice Salad.

Memorable backpacking meals deserve a special dessert—because you're special, and you deserve it. There are plenty of ways to create them in Chapter Ten: Baked Pumpkin-Spice Apples, Grated Apples with Lemon Juice, Tortilla Fruit Tarts, Peach Granola Clusters, Hot Peach Crumble, Watermelon Treats, Banana Pudding, Blueberry-Apple Fruit Leather & Pudding, and Baked Sweet Potato Pudding with Glazed Pecan Sauce. You might want to start with this chapter first.

Chapter Eleven wraps up the book with tips for drying, storing, and packing food. You'll find tips to reduce the problem of vacuum-sealed bags losing their seals due to contact with the sharp edges of dried foods. With proper handling, the meals you take to the trail will reward you with great taste, appearance, and nutrition.

Thank you to everyone who has purchased the *Recipes for Adventure* books and to the readers of *Trail Bytes*. Your encouraging words to "keep up the good work" made this project possible.

Bon appétit.

Chef Glenn

# 1. Breakfast Recipes

## Omelet Bites

When eggs are combined with a starch before cooking and dehydrating them, they rehydrate well. Without a starch incorporated into the eggs, they remain hard. Omelet Bites use potatoes for starch, similar to Spanish omelets. Bake them in the oven, and make different types of omelets by adding 1 or 2 more ingredients to the mix.

*Rehydrated Baked Bean & Tomato Omelet Bites.*

**There are 5 recipes that follow the sections on cooking and dehydrating Omelet Bites:**

- Spanish Omelet with Onions
- Ham & Cheese
- Baked Bean & Tomato
- Broccoli & Tomato
- Sausage-Seasoned Ground Beef

### Cooking Omelet Bites

Steam 1 pound (454 g) of whole, unpeeled potatoes for 15 minutes. Then cover cooked potatoes with cold water. Once cooled, peel potatoes, and grate them coarsely. The goal is to yield 12 ounces (340 g) of grated potatoes.

Prepare/precook additional ingredients as described in the individual recipes. The quantity of additional ingredients ranges from 8 ounces (227 g) up to 1 pound (454 g).
*See **Omelet Bites Recipes**, pages 6 and 7.*

Whisk 1 pound of eggs (8–9 eggs, 454 g) in a bowl. Fold in 12 ounces of steamed, grated potatoes (340 g), plus the additional ingredients.

Preheat oven to 350°F (180°C).

Line a 12″×9″ glass baking dish with baking paper. Pour mixture into baking dish, and distribute evenly to corners.

Bake on center rack for 30 minutes, then turn off stove. Leave dish in oven for 10 more minutes.

Remove baked eggs from oven, and allow to cool. Flip eggs over onto a cutting board, and peel away baking paper.

Cut into ½-inch columns, and then ½-inch rows, so you end up with ½-inch cubes (slightly more than 1 cm).

## Dehydrating Omelet Bites

Place Omelet Bites directly on mesh sheet of dehydrator tray in a single layer with a little space between cubes.

Dehydrate at 145°F (63°C) for 6–8 hours. Dried Omelet Bites will be crunchy. Cut a few in half to make sure the insides are dry.

## Rehydrating Omelet Bites

**Regular Serving:** Rehydrate ¾ cup Omelet Bites (50 g) with ½ cup water (119 ml).

**Large Serving:** Rehydrate 1 cup Omelet Bites (70 g) with ¾ cup water (178 ml).

**Pot Cooking:** Soak Omelet Bites in water for 5 minutes, then bring to a boil for 1 minute. Transfer pot to an insulating cozy for 15 minutes.

**Thermos Cooking:** Add boiled water to ingredients in thermos. Wait 20 minutes, up to an hour. There is no need for additional water. Overnight soaking is not recommended.

# Omelet Bites Recipes

## Ham & Cheese

**SERVINGS: 3 – 4**

**INGREDIENTS:**

1 lb. eggs (8–9 eggs, 454 g)
12 oz. potatoes, steamed and grated (340 g)
8 oz. ham or Canadian bacon, precooked (227 g)
1 Tbsp. mustard
1 Tbsp. chives, dried
½ tsp. salt
¼ tsp. pepper
4 oz. cheese, any kind (added on the trail)

**Ham Prep:** Use a thick cut (approximately 1⁄4-inch) of lean, precooked ham. Canadian bacon (back bacon) is a good choice. The name is confusing because it is not really what is commonly called bacon. Regular strip bacon is too fatty to use in dehydrated meals. Dice ham into small pieces, and then mash with a kitchen mallet until the texture of the meat is shredded. Fold ham into egg-potato mixture and bake.

**Optional Ingredient:** Turn this omelet into a familiar Western omelet with 4 ounces (113 g) of finely diced green bell pepper. Fold in with the ham.

**Cheese Option:** If you carry a block of cheese, add a few slices to the cooked Omelet Bites in camp before serving. Adding the cheese too soon can make the pot harder to clean.

## Spanish Omelet with Onions

**SERVINGS: 3 – 4**

**INGREDIENTS:**

1 lb. eggs (8–9 eggs, 454 g)
12 oz. potatoes, steamed and grated (340 g)
2 medium onions (227 g)
1 Tbsp. mustard
¾ tsp. salt
¼ tsp. pepper

**Onion Prep:** Dice onions into small pieces. Lightly coat a pan with 2 teaspoons of cooking oil. Sauté onions over medium-high heat for 5 minutes until translucent but not browned. Fold onions into egg-potato mixture and bake.

Note: Omelet Bites with onions may take an hour longer than other Omelet Bites to dehydrate.

## Broccoli & Tomato

**SERVINGS: 3 – 4**

**INGREDIENTS:**

1 lb. eggs (8–9 eggs, 454 g)
12 oz. potatoes, steamed and grated (340 g)
5 oz. broccoli florets, steamed (142 g)
2 medium tomatoes, diced (227 g)
1 Tbsp. mustard
1 tsp. chives, dried
¾ tsp. salt
¼ tsp. pepper
¼ tsp. thyme, dried

**Broccoli Prep:** Cut florets into smaller pieces and steam for 5 minutes. Combine steamed broccoli and diced tomatoes with all seasonings, then fold into egg-potato mixture, and bake.

## Sausage-Seasoned Ground Beef

**SERVINGS: 3 – 4**

**INGREDIENTS:**

1 lb. eggs (8–9 eggs, 454 g)

12 oz. potatoes, steamed and grated (340 g)

8 oz. lean ground beef, sausage seasoned and cooked (227 g)

*See **Sausage-Seasoned Ground Beef**, page 58.*

**Ground Beef Prep:** Use only lean ground beef with fat content not exceeding the 7–10 percent range.

Work the seasoned breadcrumbs or ground oats into ½ pound of raw ground beef (227 g). Form the meat into a big meatball, and let it sit in the refrigerator for 15 minutes. Then, pull the meat apart into small pieces for cooking.

Begin frying meat at medium-low temperature to release a little grease. That way, you won't have to use any cooking oil. After the pan looks a little moist, increase the temperature to medium high. Stir meat continuously until the meat is lightly browned inside and out, about 10 minutes. Finally, blot off any grease with paper towels, although there won't be much grease if you use lean ground beef.

Fold cooked ground beef into egg-potato mixture and bake.

## Baked Bean & Tomato

**SERVINGS: 3 – 4**

**INGREDIENTS:**

1 lb. eggs (8–9 eggs, 454 g)

12 oz. potatoes, steamed and grated (340 g)

8 oz. vegetarian baked beans (227 g)

2 medium tomatoes, diced (227 g)

1 Tbsp. mustard

1 tsp. salt

1 tsp. parsley, dried

½ tsp. marjoram, dried

½ tsp. basil, dried

¼ tsp. onion powder

¼ tsp. pepper

**Baked Bean Prep:** Drain baked beans in a colander, but don't rinse.

**Tomato Prep:** Dice ripe tomatoes. If using canned diced tomatoes, drain off sauce or liquid from the can. Add all of the seasonings to the diced tomatoes.

Combine tomatoes and beans, then fold into the egg-potato mixture and bake.

*(Left) Sausage-Seasoned Ground Beef Omelet Bites; (Right) Baked Bean & Tomato Omelet Bites.*

# Tortilla Grits Bowl & Raspberry Roll-Up

Push an 8-inch tortilla into a bowl, which will require overlapping the tortilla in two places. The photos show 1 of the bowls that comes with a GSI-Dualist Cookset. This tortilla trick will also work with collapsible bowls. Fill tortilla bowl with grits and top with cheese.

When round 1 of breakfast is over, spread a packet or two of raspberry jam on the tortilla and fold it up. Alternatively, heat and rehydrate dried fruit or fruit leather while you're eating the grits.

## Easy Grits Recipe

Fine-ground grits cook faster than coarse-ground grits, with no need to precook and dehydrate. Finely ground grits are often labeled as "polenta." Some of the germ is removed in processing. Instant grits, on the other hand, have had the entire germ removed. Instant grits may be used if desired.

This recipe includes dried meat. *See dehydrating* ***Canadian bacon bits*** *on page 69, or dehydrating* ***sausage-seasoned ground beef*** *on page 58.*

**Regular Serving:** ¼ cup fine-ground grits (45 g), ¼ cup dried meat (25 g), 1 oz. fresh cheese (28 g), and 1½ cups water to cook (355 ml).

**Large Serving:** ⅓ cup fine-ground grits (60 g), ⅓ cup dried meat (35 g), 1½ oz. fresh cheese (43 g), and 2 cups water to cook (473 ml).

Pack grits and dried meat in separate bags.

Soak dried meat in water for 5 minutes, then bring to a boil. Stir in grits and transfer pot to an insulating cozy for 15 minutes. Top with cheese when serving.

If you eat your grits in a separate bowl, slosh some water around in the pot while you're eating to keep any residual starch from drying in the pot. For a unique breakfast, with no additional cleanup, serve grits in a tortilla bowl.

# Overnight Bircher Muesli: A No-Cook Breakfast

Overnight muesli saves fuel and time while providing a nourishing cold breakfast. A thermos food jar works well to soak the oats and dried fruit overnight, but any sealable food container will work.

There are no firm rules for making Bircher Muesli, except for using soaked rolled oats and grated apples. To those ingredients, add other fruits, berries, nuts, and seeds.

**SERVINGS: 1 LARGE**

**INGREDIENTS:**

½ cup rolled oats (50 g)

½ cup dried grated apples (16 g), equivalent to 1 small apple *(See **dehydrating grated apples**, page 106)*

⅛ cup dried bananas (10 g), equivalent to ⅓ of a banana

¼ cup dried mixed berries (10 g) *(See **dehydrating berries**, page 114)*

Toppings: walnut pieces, tsp. sugar, pinch cinnamon

**Optional:** 4 Tbsp. powdered milk, makes 8 oz. (237 ml)

1½ cups cold water to rehydrate (355 ml)

**Packing:** Pack oats and dried fruit in 1 Ziploc bag. Pack toppings and milk powder in separate bags.

Combine oats and fruit with 1½ cups cold water in a thermos or other sealable container. Soak overnight or for at least 2 hours. When serving, top with walnut pieces, sugar to taste, and a pinch of cinnamon. Mix up 1 cup of milk and pour as much as you like over the finished muesli.

**Alternative:** For a hot breakfast, add fruit to water, bring to boil, then add to oats in thermos or pot.

# Pancake Bites

Pancake Bites are baked in the oven without dairy ingredients or eggs and then dried. They rehydrate quickly and taste great with dried fruits or berries.

**SERVINGS: 4 – 6**

**INGREDIENTS:**

1 ½ cups flour (200 g)
½ cup ground rolled oats (50 g)
1 ½ Tbsp. Baking powder (16 g)
1 Tbsp. ground flax seeds + 3 Tbsp. water
1 Tbsp. sugar (15 g)
1 tsp. salt (6 g)
½ tsp. cinnamon
1 banana, mashed (100 g)*
1 Tbsp. maple syrup
1 ¼ cups almond milk (296 ml)
½ Tbsp. cooking oil (to grease baking dish)

* ½ cup of applesauce or pureed pumpkin (100 g) may be used in place of banana for variety.

## Cooking Pancake Bites

Preheat oven to 350°F (180°C).

In a small bowl, combine 1 tablespoon of freshly ground flax seeds with 3 tablespoons of water. Stir and set aside. Mixture will become gel-like within 10 minutes, which serves as a binder in baking.

Combine all other dry ingredients in a large bowl.

Hand-mash a banana on a plate until smooth, like baby food.

Add almond milk to dry ingredients and whisk until combined.

Stir in mashed banana, ground flax seed mixture, and maple syrup.

Coat bottom and lower sides of a 12″×9″ glass or ceramic baking dish with ½ tablespoon of cooking oil. Add pancake mixture.

Place in preheated oven on middle rack. Bake for 30 minutes at 350°F (180°C). Turn the baking dish halfway through if your oven does not bake evenly. The top of the pancakes will turn light brown. Remove from oven and let cool.

## Dehydrating Pancake Bites

Once pancakes are cool enough to work with, cut into 4 sections. Run a spatula under the pancakes to remove the sections from the baking dish. Cut each section into cubes about an inch square.

Place cubes directly on mesh sheet of dehydrator tray. This recipe will fill 1 Excalibur Dehydrator tray.

Dehydrate at 135°F (57°C) for 4–6 hours or until crunchy.

**Yield:** Approximately 12.6 ounces (300 g) dried Pancake Bites.

**Packing:** Pack dried fruit and pancake bites in separate bags.

**Regular Serving:** ¼ cup dried fruit (20 g), 1.8 oz. Pancake Bites (50 g), and ¾ cup water to rehydrate (177 ml).

**Large Serving:** ⅓ cup dried fruit (25 g), 2.6 oz. Pancake Bites (75 g), and 1 cup water to rehydrate (237 ml).

Pancake Bites are bulky; it's more accurate to measure them by weight, rather than volume.

## Rehydrating Pancake Bites

Combine dried fruit and water in pot and soak for 5 minutes. Bring fruit to a boil. Add Pancake Bites to pot on top of fruit, but don't stir them in. Put lid on pot and continue cooking for a few more seconds to build up steam. Turn off stove, and wait 10 minutes. Then, stir Pancake Bites and fruit together to serve.

*Pancake Bites with dried apples and apricots*

## Cream of Pancakes

Grind Pancake Bites into powder using a blender. More water is used to rehydrate cream of pancakes than regular Pancake Bites. The cereal rehydrates almost instantly.

**Regular Serving:** ¼ cup dried fruit (20 g), ⅓ cup ground Pancake Bites (50 g), and 1⅓ cups water to rehydrate (316 ml).

**Large Serving:** ⅓ cup dried fruit (25 g), ½ cup ground Pancake Bites (75 g), and 2 cups water to rehydrate (473 ml).

**Optional Ingredients:** ¼ cup pecan or walnut pieces (30 g), and 2 Tbsp. powdered milk.

**Packing:** Pack dried fruit, nuts, ground pancakes, and milk powder in separate bags.

## Rehydrating Cream of Pancakes

Combine dried fruit and water in pot and soak for 5 minutes. Bring fruit to a boil. Stir in ground pancakes and nut pieces, and turn off stove. Insulate pot for 5 to 10 minutes.

This creamy cereal tastes great with milk. In a separate container, stir 2 tablespoons of powdered milk into ½ cup of water. Pour milk over cereal when serving.

# 2. Soup Recipes

## Cream of Cauliflower Soup

**SERVINGS: 4–5**

**INGREDIENTS:**

1 large head cauliflower
4 medium carrots
3 medium potatoes
1 medium onion
1 clove garlic
1 Tbsp. vegetable bouillon (15 g)
1 tsp. salt
¼ tsp. pepper
⅛ tsp. ground cloves
5 cups water (1183 ml)

### Cooking Cream of Cauliflower Soup

Wash cauliflower, and cut into chunks. Discard tough portion of the lower stem. Peel and grate potatoes and carrots. Dice onions and mince garlic.

In a large stockpot, cook onions and garlic for 5 minutes using minimal oil.

Add grated carrots, potatoes, and seasonings. Continue cooking for another 5 minutes, stirring frequently. Add some of the water if necessary.

Add cauliflower and water. Bring to a boil, then reduce to a simmer for 20 minutes.

Run the soup through a blender. It will take 2 fills for most blenders.

If not dehydrating, stir in a little half-and-half. For style points, top with chives or parsley and perhaps a sprinkle of paprika.

### Dehydrating Cream of Cauliflower Soup

Spread cooled soup thinly on dehydrator trays. If using an Excalibur Dehydrator, 1.5 cups of blended soup is a good quantity per tray.

Dehydrate at 135°F (57°C) for 10–12 hours. Dried soup bark will be brittle. Reduce soup bark to powder in a blender.

### Rehydrating Cream of Cauliflower Soup

**1 Serving:** Combine 4 tablespoons of soup powder (48 g) with 2 cups (473 ml) of boiled water. Stir and insulate pot for 15 minutes, or enjoy soup up to several hours later if rehydrating in a thermos.

# Vegetable-Soup Powder

**SERVINGS: 15 TBSP. SOUP POWDER. MAKES 7–8 CUPS RECONSTITUTED SOUP.**

**INGREDIENTS:**

5–6 celery stalks (250 g)
7–8 medium carrots (350 g)
2 small onions (100 g)
3 cloves garlic (20 g)
5–6 small potatoes (450 g)
2 Tbsp. tomato paste (35 g)
2 tsp. soy sauce
1 Tbsp. apple-cider vinegar
1 thick slice lemon
2 tsp. cooking oil
5 cups water (1183 ml)

**Dry Seasonings:**

1½ tsp. salt
¼ tsp. pepper
½ tsp. parsley
½ tsp. sage
½ tsp. rosemary
½ tsp. thyme
2 bay leaves

## Cooking Vegetable Soup

Dice the celery and onions, and mince the garlic.

Peel and grate the carrots.

Peel and grate the potatoes.

Combine dry seasonings in a bowl, and rub them between your fingers to let the flavors meld.

Coat the bottom of large soup pot with 2 teaspoons of cooking oil. Begin sautéing celery and onions on medium heat. Add garlic after 5 minutes, and stir continuously for another minute.

Add the carrots, tomato paste, lemon slice, soy sauce, and all dry seasonings. When ingredients are well combined and steaming, add the potatoes.

Stir for a minute, and then add the water and bay leaves. Bring to a boil, and then reduce heat to maintain a low simmer. Continue cooking on low with lid on pot for 20 minutes.

Remove pot from heat, stir in the vinegar, and allow soup to cool.

Pick out the bay leaves and lemon slice, then run the soup through a blender.

## Dehydrating Vegetable Soup

Dehydrate at 135°F (57°C) for 10–12 hours.

Spread soup thinly on dehydrator trays covered with nonstick sheets. If using an Excalibur Dehydrator, that will amount to approximately 1⅓ cups on each of 5 trays.

Dried soup will easily tear into small pieces. Reduce the pieces to powder in a blender.

**Wet Yield:** Approximately 7 cups (1.66 L) of wet soup before drying.

**Dry Yield:** Approximately 15 tablespoons (180 g) of soup power (12 g each).

## Rehydrating Vegetable Soup

**Pot Cooking:** Add 2 tablespoons (24 g) of soup powder per cup (237 ml) of water. A good serving size is 2 cups (473 ml) of water with 4 tablespoons (48 g) of soup powder. Bring to a boil, and then remove pot from heat and transfer to an insulating cozy. Wait 15 minutes before serving. Stir to thicken. Soup will thicken with more time.

**Thermos Cooking:** Add boiled water to soup powder in same quantities as above. Shake and wait 30 minutes or more.

**Extra Ingredients:** This vegetable-soup base will support the addition of virtually any combination of dried meats, beans, leafy greens, or vegetables. Try this blend: 4 tablespoons soup powder (48 g), ¾ cup extra ingredients (60 g), 2¾ cups (650 ml) boiled water.

*(Left) Ingredients used to make Chicken-Vegetable Noodle Soup: ¼ cup dried ground chicken, ¼ cup dried mixed vegetables, ¼ cup dried linguine noodles, 4 Tbsp. vegetable-soup powder; (Right) rehydrated Chicken-Vegetable Noodle Soup.*

## Combining Soup Powders

(Left to right) Tomato-Carrot Soup powder, Potato-Broccoli-Soup powder, and Vegetable-Soup powder.

Create a wide variety of soup stocks by mixing different soup powders together instead of using just 1.

**Here are some examples to make 2 cups of stock (473 ml):**

1 Tbsp. Vegetable-Soup powder + 3 Tbsp. ***Potato-Broccoli-Soup powder,*** page 16.
2 Tbsp. Vegetable-Soup powder + 2 Tbsp. ***Tomato-Carrot-Soup powder,*** page 18.
3 Tbsp. Vegetable-Soup powder + 1 Tbsp. ***Curry-Carrot-Soup powder,*** page 20.

*Tortellini Soup made with 2 Tbsp. Vegetable-Soup powder and 2 Tbsp. Tomato-Carrot-Soup powder. Extra ingredients: ⅓ cup dried tortellini and ⅓ cup dried mixed-vegetables (red and yellow bell peppers and green beans). Water to rehydrate: 2⅔ cups.*

## Add Soup Powders to Dehydrated Meals

Instead of using bouillon cubes, add a couple tablespoons of soup powder to dehydrated meals. Increase the rehydration water by ¼–½ cup, depending on how saucy you want the meal to be. It will create a flavorful sauce to go with the starches, meats, and vegetables.

# Potato-Broccoli Soup

**SERVINGS: 7–8 CUPS**

**INGREDIENTS:**

1½ lb. broccoli florets (680 g)
1 lb. potatoes (453 g)
1–2 medium carrots (100 g)
1 medium onion (75 g)
2 cloves garlic
1 tsp. cooking oil
¼ cup pickle juice (60 ml)
4 cups water (946 ml)

**Dry Seasonings:**

1½ tsp. salt
¼ tsp. ground pepper
½ tsp. parsley
½ tsp. thyme

## Cooking Potato-Broccoli Soup

It takes 4 heads of broccoli to produce 680 grams of florets. Using only florets helps keep the soup green. Stems turn brown during dehydration.

Dice the onion, and mince the garlic. Peel and slice the carrots thinly.

Peel the potatoes and cut into small chunks. Place them in a bowl of water, then drain off water when you add them to the soup. This reduces starch and prevents the potatoes from browning.

Coat the bottom of large soup pot with a teaspoon of cooking oil. Sauté onions on medium heat. Add garlic after 5 minutes, stirring continuously for 1 minute. Add the carrots, all of the dry seasonings, plus one cup of water. Continue cooking for another 5 minutes.

Add potatoes to the pot and the remaining 3 cups of water. Bring to a boil, and then reduce heat to a simmer for 10 minutes.

Add broccoli florets and continue simmering soup for 5 minutes.

Take soup off the heat and stir in the pickle juice.

Let soup cool and run it through a blender.

## Dehydrating Potato-Broccoli Soup

Dehydrate at 135°F (57°C) for 10–12 hours.

This recipe yields approximately 7½ cups (1774 ml) of wet soup before drying.

Spread soup thinly on dehydrator trays covered with nonstick sheets. If using an Excalibur dehydrator, that will amount to approximately 1½ cups on each of 5 trays. If you have more trays available, spread soup thinner. Remove nonstick sheets when soup is almost dry.

Dried soup will easily crumble into small pieces.

Reduce the pieces to powder in a blender.

**Dry Yield:** Approximately 15 tablespoons (180 g) of soup power (12 grams each).

## Rehydrating Potato-Broccoli Soup

**Pot Cooking:** Add 2 tablespoons (24 g) of soup powder per cup of water. Two cups (473 ml) of water with 4 tablespoons (48 g) of soup powder is a good serving size. Bring to a boil, and then remove pot from heat and transfer to an insulating pot cozy. Wait 10–15 minutes before serving. Stir to thicken. Soup will thicken with more time.

**Thermos Cooking:** Add boiled water to soup powder in same quantities as above. Shake and wait 30 minutes or more.

**Extra Ingredients:** Broccoli potato soup combines well with dried ground beef or ham, plus any colorful dried vegetables such as carrots or corn. Try this blend: 4 Tbsp. soup powder (48 g), ⅓ cup extra ingredients (24 g), 2⅓ cups boiled water (550 ml).

# Tomato-Carrot Soup

**SERVINGS: 6–7 CUPS**

**INGREDIENTS:**

3½ lb. ripe tomatoes (1587 g)
1 lb. carrots (453 g)
1 small sweet potato (227 g)
1 celery stalk (50 g)
¼ lb. pickled beets (100 g)
¼ cup pickled beet juice (60 ml)
2 small onions (75 g)
1 clove garlic
1 thick slice lemon
2 tsp. cooking oil

**Dry Seasonings:**

2 tsp. herbs de Provence
1 tsp. basil
1½ tsp. salt
¼ tsp. pepper
½ tsp. ground cumin
¼ tsp. chili mix powder
1 bay leaf

## Cooking Tomato-Carrot Soup

Finely dice the celery and onions, and mince the garlic.

Peel and thinly slice the carrots.

Peel and cut sweet potato into small cubes. Place sweet potato cubes in a bowl with water, then drain off water when ready to add cubes to the soup. This will prevent browning.

Process the tomatoes by removing the fibrous white pith from the centers, but leave the seeds. Cut tomatoes into small chunks, capturing the juices too.

Cut pickled beets into small pieces.

Combine all dry seasonings, except the bay leaf, in a small bowl, and rub them between your fingers to let the flavors meld.

Coat the bottom of a large soup pot with 2 teaspoons of cooking oil. Begin sautéing celery and onions on medium heat. Add garlic after 5 minutes, and stir continuously for another minute. Add the tomatoes, pickled beets, and pickled beet juice. Increase heat to medium high. Once boiling, add the carrots, sweet potato cubes, lemon slice, and bay leaf. Return to a boil, and then maintain a low simmer for 30 minutes.

Allow soup to cool, remove lemon slice and bay leaf, then run the soup through a blender

*Soup spread thinly on nonstick sheet; Soup leather flipped, nonstick sheet removed.*

## Dehydrating Tomato-Carrot Soup

Dehydrate at 135°F (57°C) for 10–12 hours.

**Wet Yield:** Approximately 6¾ cups (1597 ml) of wet soup before drying.

Spread soup thinly on dehydrator trays covered with nonstick sheets. If using an Excalibur Dehydrator, that will amount to approximately 1⅓ cups on each of 5 trays.

Dried soup will easily tear into small pieces. Reduce the pieces to powder in a blender.

**Dry Yield:** Approximately 16 tablespoons (192 g) of soup power (12 g each).

## Rehydrating Tomato-Carrot Soup

Add 2 tablespoons (24 g) of soup powder per cup (237 ml) of water.

**Regular Serving:** 3 Tbsp. soup powder (36 g), 1½ cups water (355 ml).

**Large Serving:** 4 Tbsp. soup powder (48 g), 2 cups water (473 ml).

**Pot Cooking:** Combine soup powder with water. Soak for 5 minutes, and then bring to a boil for 1 minute. Transfer pot to an insulating cozy for 15 minutes.

**Thermos Cooking:** Add boiled water to ingredients in thermos. Wait 20 minutes, up to several hours. Use ¼ cup extra boiled water for longer soak times; soup thickens.

**Extra Ingredients:** This tomato-carrot-soup base will support the addition of virtually any combination of dried meats, beans, leafy greens, or any colorful vegetables. Try this blend: 4 Tbsp. soup powder (48 g), ⅓ cup extra ingredients (24 g), 2⅓ cups boiled water (550 ml).

# Curry-Carrot Soup

## SERVINGS: 6–7 CUPS

### INGREDIENTS:

1½ lb. carrots (680 g)
¾ lb. sweet potatoes (340 g)
1 medium onion (125 g)
3 cloves garlic (20 g)
2 Tbsp. tomato paste (35 g)
2 tsp. cooking oil
4 cups water (946 ml)

**Dry Seasonings:**

3 Tbsp. curry powder
1½ tsp. salt
¼ tsp. pepper
1 tsp. ground ginger
½ tsp. red pepper flakes
½ tsp. paprika

## Cooking Curry-Carrot Soup

Dice the onions, and mince the garlic.

Peel and slice the carrots thinly.

Peel and cut sweet potatoes into small cubes. Place sweet potato cubes in a bowl with water, then drain off water when ready to add cubes to the soup. This will prevent browning.

Combine all dry seasonings in a small bowl.

Coat the bottom of a large soup pot with 2 teaspoons of cooking oil. Begin sautéing onions on medium heat.

Add garlic after 5 minutes, and stir continuously for another minute.

Add the carrots, tomato paste, and all dry seasonings. When ingredients are well combined and steaming, add the sweet potato cubes and 4 cups of water.

Bring to a boil, and then reduce heat to maintain a low simmer. Continue cooking on low with lid on pot for 20 minutes.

Remove pot from heat, and allow the soup to cool.

Run the cooled soup through a blender.

**Wet Yield:** Approximately 6½ cups (1538 ml) of wet soup before drying.

## Dehydrating Curry-Carrot Soup

Spread soup thinly on dehydrator trays covered with nonstick sheets. If using an Excalibur Dehydrator, that will amount to approximately 1¼ cups on each of 5 trays.

Dehydrate at 135°F (57°C) for 10–12 hours or until dry and crumbly.

Dried soup will easily tear or crumble into small pieces. Reduce the pieces to powder in a blender.

Dried Yield: Approximately 18 tablespoons (216 g) of soup power (12 g each).

*Dried Curry-Carrot Soup before blending into powder.*

## Rehydrating Curry-Carrot Soup

Add 2 Tbsp. (24 g) of soup powder per cup (237 ml) of water.

**Regular Serving:** 3 Tbsp. soup powder (36 g), 1½ cups water (355 ml).

**Large Serving:** 4 Tbsp. soup powder (48 g), 2 cups water (473 ml).

**Pot Cooking:** Combine soup powder with water. Soak for 5 minutes, and then bring to a boil for 1 minute. Transfer pot to an insulating cozy for 15 minutes.

**Thermos Cooking:** Add boiled water to ingredients in thermos. Wait 20 minutes, up to several hours. Use ¼ cup extra boiled water for longer soak times; soup thickens.

**Extra Ingredients:** This vegetable-soup base will support the addition of virtually any combination of dried meats, beans, tofu, or vegetables. Try this blend: 4 Tbsp. soup powder (48 g), ⅓ cup extra ingredients (24 g), 2⅓ cups boiled water (550 ml).

# Potato-Leek Soup

**SERVINGS: 6–7 (13 CUPS)**

**INGREDIENTS:**

3¾ lb. potatoes, peeled and chunked (1.7 kg)

½ lb. leeks (6 layers of a leek, cut into small pieces) (227 g)

11 cups chicken or veg. broth, or water with bouillon (2.6 L)

4 cloves garlic, minced

1 tsp. salt

¼ tsp. pepper

1 tsp. thyme, fresh preferred

3 bay leaves

2 tsp. cooking oil

½ cup half-and-half (added for immediate serving, not for dehydration)

## Cooking Potato-Leek Soup

Peel and chunk potatoes, and add to a large soup pot with salt and pepper, bay leaves, and thyme. Add enough chicken or vegetable broth to cover potatoes by half an inch. Bring to a boil, and then reduce heat to a simmer. Retain the rest of the broth.

Cut 6 to 8 layers from a leek and wash thoroughly. Remove tips if dried out, but otherwise use both the dark green and lighter parts of the leek. Slice lengthwise into thinner strips and then across into small pieces.

Add leeks and minced garlic to a frying pan coated with 2 teaspoons of cooking oil, and cook over medium heat. While the leeks are cooking, add broth to the pan ¼ cup at a time to keep the leeks from burning. By adding broth, no additional oil is needed.

When the leeks are soft after about 10 minutes, add to the soup pot with the potatoes, and simmer for an additional 10 minutes. Remove from heat, and let it cool.

Remove bay leaves, and run the soup through a blender until smooth. This may take 2 to 3 loads; an extra pot will be helpful to hold the soup as it comes out of the blender.

If serving immediately, thin soup with half-and-half and broth to desired consistency, and reheat soup.

## Dehydrating Potato-Leek Soup

Spread thinly on dehydrator trays covered with nonstick sheets or fruit-roll inserts.

Dehydrate at 135°F (57°C) for 6–8 hours or until brittle.

To speed up drying and to thoroughly dry the underside of the soup bark, flip the bark over when it is almost dry, and peel away the nonstick sheets. Finish drying directly on mesh sheets.

Break soup bark into smaller pieces when dry. For faster rehydration, grind bark into powder.

**Yield:** 13 cups of soup will yield 7–8 cups of bark. One cup of bark weighs approximately 48 grams. One cup of bark can be reduced to ¼ cup (4 Tbsp) powdered soup, also 48 grams.

*Rehydrated Potato-Leek Soup.*

## Rehydrating Potato-Leek Soup

Add 2 Tbsp. (24 g) of soup powder per cup (237 ml) of water.

**Regular Serving:** 3 Tbsp. soup powder (36 g), 1½ cups water (355 ml).

**Large Serving:** 4 Tbsp. soup powder (48 g), 2 cups water (473 ml).

**Pot Cooking:** Add ingredients to pot with water, and soak 5 minutes. Bring to boil for 1 minute, then transfer pot to an insulating cozy for 15 minutes.

**Thermos Cooking:** Add boiled water to ingredients in thermos. Wait 20 minutes, up to several hours. Use a little extra boiled water for longer soak times; soup thickens.

# Butternut Squash Soup

**SERVINGS: 3–4**

**INGREDIENTS:**

1 butternut squash, 2¼ lb. (1 kg)
1 medium onion, diced (100 g)
2 cloves garlic, minced
½ Tbsp. fresh ginger, minced
2 tsp. cooking oil
1 tsp. dried sage
1 tsp. dried rosemary
¾ tsp. salt
¼ tsp. pepper
¼ tsp. cumin
¼ tsp. turmeric
4 cups water with vegetable bouillon (946 ml)

## Cooking Butternut Squash Soup

Dissolve a vegetable bouillon cube in 4 cups of warm water.

Peel and cut butternut squash into cubes. Dice onion; mince garlic and ginger.

Coat the bottom of a large soup pot with 2 teaspoons of cooking oil. Cook onions, stirring frequently. Add spoonfuls of the vegetable stock to onions to keep them from burning. After 10 to 15 minutes, the onions will be nicely caramelized.

Add garlic and ginger, and continue cooking another 5 minutes.

Add the butternut squash and all seasonings with a little of the vegetable stock to coat. Stir together for 5 minutes, then add the rest of the vegetable stock.

Bring to a boil, then cover, and reduce heat to a low simmer for 20 minutes.

Once soup has cooled, run it through a blender until smooth.

**Wet Yield:** 5–6 cups of blended soup, depending on size of squash used.

*Rehydrated serving of Butternut Squash Soup.*

*(Left) Butternut Squash Soup spread thinly on Excalibur Dehydrator tray; (Right) dried soup flipped over directly on mesh sheet, nonstick sheet removed.*

## Dehydrating Butternut Squash Soup

Spread blended butternut soup thinly on dehydrator trays covered with nonstick sheets. If using an Excalibur Dehydrator, 1¼ cups is a good quantity to spread on a tray.

Dehydrate at 135°F (57°C) for 10–12 hours. After 9 hours, when the soup is nearly dry, flip the trays over, peel off the nonstick sheets, and continue drying directly on the mesh sheets. Dried Butternut Squash Soup will be brittle and easy to snap into smaller pieces.

Break dried soup bark into smaller pieces and grind into powder in a blender.

**Dry Yield:** Between 11 and 13 tablespoons of soup powder.

## Rehydrating Butternut Squash Soup

**Regular Serving:** 3 Tbsp. soup powder (36 g), 1½ cups water (355 ml).

**Large Serving:** 4 Tbsp. soup powder (48 g), 2 cups water (473 ml).

**Pot Cooking:** Combine soup powder with water. Soak for 5 minutes, and then bring to a boil for 1 minute. Transfer pot to an insulating cozy for 15 minutes.

**Thermos Cooking:** Add boiled water to ingredients in thermos. Wait 20 minutes, up to several hours. Use ¼ cup extra boiled water for longer soak times; soup thickens.

# Sweet Potato & Carrot Soup

Warm spices turn this sweet potato soup from mellow to marvelous. Reduce to powder after dehydration. Rehydrates in minutes into a thick, creamy soup.

**SERVINGS: 3–4**

**INGREDIENTS:**

1¾ lb. sweet potatoes (800 g)
¾ lb. carrots (340 g)
5 cups vegetable broth (1183 ml)
1 medium onion (100 g)
2 cloves garlic
1 Tbsp. fresh ginger
1 tsp. curry powder
¾ tsp. salt
½ tsp. turmeric
¼ tsp. paprika
¼ tsp. pepper
¼ tsp. cinnamon
2 tsp. cooking oil

## Cooking Sweet Potato & Carrot Soup

Peel sweet potatoes and carrots, and cut them into small pieces. Dice onion, and mince garlic and ginger.

Coat a large soup pot with 2 teaspoons cooking oil. Cook onions on medium-high heat, stirring frequently, for 10 minutes. Add spoonfuls of vegetable broth to keep the onions from scorching. Reduce heat, and add garlic, ginger, all spices, and more broth as needed. Cook about 5 minutes.

Add sweet potatoes, carrots, and vegetable broth. Bring to a boil, then cover, and reduce to a simmer for 30 minutes. Allow soup to cool, then run it through a blender.

**Wet Yield:** Approximately 7¼ cups of blended soup (1.7 L).

*Sweet Potato & Carrot Soup dried into bark and then ground into powder.*

## Dehydrating Sweet Potato & Carrot Soup

Spread blended soup thinly on dehydrator trays covered with nonstick sheets. If using an Excalibur Dehydrator with 5 trays, spread slightly more than 1⅓ cups per tray.

Dehydrate at 135°F (57°C) for 12–14 hours.

After 10 hours, when the soup is nearly dry, flip the trays over, peel off the nonstick sheets, and continue drying directly on the mesh sheets. Dried soup is brittle.

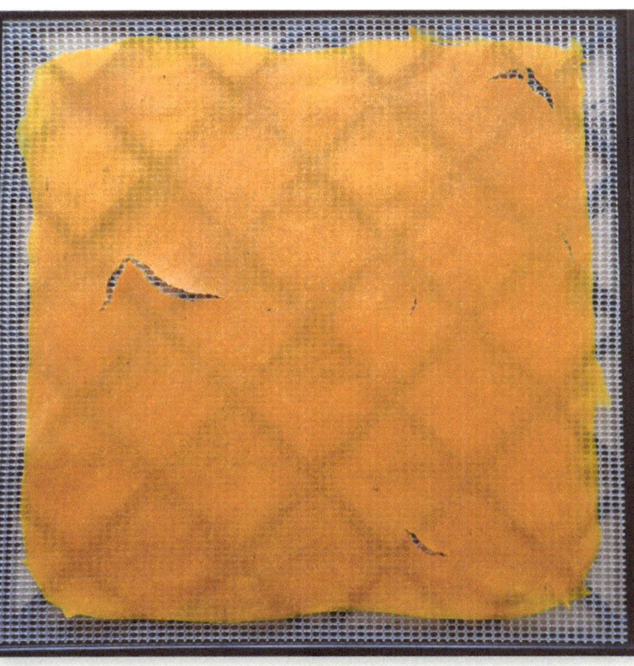

*(Left) Wet soup spread thinly on tray; (right) almost-dried soup shown flipped over with nonstick sheet pulled away.*

Once dry, break soup bark into pieces, and grind into powder using a blender.

**Dry Yield:** Approximately 24 tablespoons of soup powder.

## Rehydrating Sweet Potato & Carrot Soup

**Regular Serving:** 6 Tbsp. soup powder, 1½ cups water (355 ml).

**Large Serving:** 8 Tbsp. soup powder, 2 cups water (473 ml).

**Pot Cooking:** Combine soup powder with water. Soak for 5 minutes, and then bring to a boil for 1 minute. Transfer pot to an insulating cozy for 15 minutes.

**Thermos Cooking:** Add boiled water to ingredients in thermos. Wait 20 minutes, up to several hours. Use ¼ cup extra boiled water for longer soak times; soup thickens.

# Fish Chowder

To make this meal without dehydrating it, use a few tablespoons of butter, instead of oil, to cook the onion and celery. Also, before serving, add 1 or 2 cups of milk. Keep the stove on after adding the milk to heat it up, but don't heat it so much that it boils. Leave out the butter and milk if dehydrating, since dairy foods won't keep long in storage.

**SERVINGS: 5 SERVINGS, 2 CUPS EACH**

**INGREDIENTS:**

2 tsp. cooking oil

1 large onion (1 cup, diced)

4 stalks celery (1 cup, diced)

4 large carrots (1½ cups, sliced)

8 medium red potatoes (4 cups, diced)

2 lb. frozen cod or white fish, thawed and cut into small chunks (.9 kg)

2 tsp. salt

½ tsp. pepper

1 tsp. Old Bay Seasoning (or similar fish seasoning)

3 bay leaves

4 cups water (946 ml)

## Cooking Fish Chowder

Cook onion and celery using minimal cooking oil in pot over medium heat, about 5 minutes.

Add carrots, potatoes, all seasonings, and 4 cups of water to pot. Increase heat until boiling, then reduce to low, and simmer for 10 minutes.

Add fish, return to boil, then reduce heat again, and simmer for 10 more minutes.

If serving immediately, add the milk after the fish has cooked, and heat just until hot. Let the pot sit off the stove with the lid on for 15 minutes before serving. That's a good time to warm some fresh bread in the oven. As mentioned at the top, omit the milk if dehydrating the chowder.

*Fish Chowder rehydrated on the trail.*

## Dehydrating Fish Chowder

Remove 6 cups of chowder from the pot, and blend it, but leave most of the carrots in the pot. Stir the blended portion back into the unblended chowder. This will thicken the chowder enough so that it won't run off the dehydrator trays.

*(Left) 2 cups of chowder on dehydrator tray; (right) dried fish chowder.*

Spread chowder on dehydrator trays covered with nonstick sheets. This recipe produces 10 cups of chowder. If using an Excalibur Dehydrator, spread 2 cups per tray. A good serving size is 2 cups, so drying this quantity on each tray makes it easy to transfer the dried results directly into individual storage bags. For smaller dehydrators, spread less chowder per tray for efficient drying.

Dehydrate at 145°F (63°C) for 12–14 hours or until completely dry and crumbly.

Flip the chowder over after 8 hours to expose the bottom of the drying chowder to more air circulation. To flip an Excalibur tray, place a nonstick sheet over the tray with the food on it. On top of that, place a mesh sheet and tray. Squeeze the 3 trays together, and turn them over so that the dried food is now bottom-side up.

## Rehydrating Fish Chowder

**Regular Serving:** 1 cup dried Fish Chowder (55 g), 1 cup water (237 ml).

**Large Serving:** 1½ cups dried Fish Chowder (82 g), 1½ cups water (355 ml).

**Pot Cooking:** Combine dried chowder and water in pot. Soak 5 minutes, and then bring to a boil for 1 minute. Transfer pot to an insulating cozy for 15 minutes.

**Thermos Cooking:** Use ¼–½ cup more water than amounts above used for pot cooking. Regular Serving: 1¼ cups water (295 ml). Large Serving: 2 cups water (473 ml). Add boiled water to dried chowder in thermos. Wait 20 minutes, up to several hours. Chowder thickens with time.

# Turning Dehydrated Meals into Soup

It's a good practice to use up dried food within one year and replace it with a new supply. One way to enjoy dehydrated meals at home while they are still in good condition is to turn them into soup. In an extended emergency, a single large-serving meal could be stretched into 2 or 3 servings of comforting hot soup.

In most cases, the only ingredients you need to turn a dehydrated meal into soup is a little salt and pepper, bouillon or other seasonings, and perhaps a few pinches of your favorite dried herbs.

The following soups, **Crab Marinara Soup, BBQ Beef & Vegetable Soup, and Chicken & Rice with Vegetables Soup,** are made from dried meals that were featured in *The Action Guide: Dehydrating 31 Meals.*

## Crab Marinara Soup

**Servings:** 2–3

**Meal Ingredients:** ¾ cup precooked-and-dried pasta (70 g), ⅓ cup dried mixed vegetables (20 g), ⅓ cup dried imitation crabmeat (25 g), and ⅓ cup marinara-sauce leather (25 g).

**Additional Ingredients:** ¼ tsp. salt, ⅛ tsp. pepper, ⅛ tsp. Old Bay Seasoning, Pinch each: herbs de Provence, oregano, basil, and red pepper flakes

To make it a soup, triple the rehydration water specified in the recipe. That translates to 5¼ cups of water (242 ml) instead of the usual 1¾ cups (414 ml). Naturally, the meal-turned-soup needs a few pinches of seasonings to make it tasty. With the additional seasonings, the tomato stock tastes like minestrone.

**Soup Preparation:** Soak the dried ingredients in the water for 5 minutes, then bring to a boil. Reduce to a light simmer for a few more minutes, then take the pot off the heat. For best results, let the soup sit covered for 30 minutes or more off the heat. Adjust seasonings and reheat prior to serving.

## BBQ Beef & Vegetable Soup

**Servings:** 2–3

**Meal Ingredients:** ¾ cup BBQ potato bark (55 g), ⅓ cup dried mixed vegetables (25 g), ⅓ cup dried ground beef (40 g).

Since BBQ potato bark already has a pretty intense flavor, all that is needed to turn it into a soup is a few shakes of salt and pepper.

**Soup Preparation:** Combine dried ingredients with 5 to 6 cups of water, or more, depending on how thick you want it. Potato bark makes a thick soup. Bring to a boil, and then simmer on low until the vegetables are well rehydrated.

**Tip:** The soup will reconstitute faster if you grind the BBQ potato bark into powder first.

## Chicken & Rice with Vegetables Soup

**Servings:** 2–3

**Meal Ingredients:** ¾ cup dried rice, chicken flavored (100 g), ⅓ cup dried ground chicken (40 g), ⅓ cup dried mixed vegetables (25 g).

**Additional Ingredients:** Salt and pepper, chicken or vegetable bouillon, or homemade vegetable soup powder, dried herbs.

**Soup Preparation:** Combine the dried meal ingredients with 5 to 6 cups of water. Bring to a boil, and then simmer until vegetables are well rehydrated. Season to taste with bouillon, herbs, salt, and pepper.

**More Soup Recipes:** ***Tofu Vegetable Soup*** on page 36, ***Beef & Barley Soup*** on page 78, and ***Barley with Peas & Mushrooms Soup*** on page 81.

# 3. Tofu Recipes

## How to Dehydrate Tofu

The secret to dehydrating tofu that rehydrates well and tastes great in meals is to freeze it first. This section explains how to dehydrate tofu in 3 important steps and then describes how to incorporate tofu into dehydrated meals for backpacking or home use.

### Step 1: Freeze It

Choose firm or extra-firm tofu. Keep the tofu in its original package, and freeze it solid. Once frozen, thaw it out overnight in the refrigerator. That way you can prep and dry it during the day.

Why is freezing tofu before drying it so important? Tofu is very dense. Freezing it opens up air spaces in the tofu through the expansion of frozen liquid inside. Dehydrating tofu, without freezing it first, results in tofu that resists rehydration. It will be rubbery and hard. Freezing also shortens the drying time because the heat and air circulation of the dehydrator can get into the air pockets.

### Step 2: Slice It Thinly

Even with freezing, tofu is still dense. It dries best when sliced into thin slabs about a ½-centimeter (less than ¼ inch) thick. Slicing tofu thinly also allows more flavor to penetrate it when you cook it before drying it.

Open package and drain off any liquid.

Slice thinly down the entire block of tofu. Then, turn the tofu a quarter turn, and cut the other way into desired shapes. This is best accomplished by dividing the block into 2 or 3 stacks. Slice into noodle shapes, or small squares (2 quarter turns). A good size for squares is 1 centimeter, or about ⅓ of an inch.

### Step 3: Add Flavor and Cook It

In the same way that rice and potatoes absorb flavors when cooked in broth before dehydrating, tofu also absorbs flavors well. The following examples show how to dehydrate tofu in vegetable bouillon, taco seasoning, and curry seasoning. When combined with other ingredients in a dehydrated meal, the captured flavors enhance the whole meal.

## Cooking Tofu with Vegetable Bouillon

*Noodle-cut tofu cooking in vegetable bouillon.*

Starting Tofu Quantity: 9 oz. (250 g).

Add 6 to 10 grams of vegetable bouillon to a pan with 8 ounces of water (236 ml). Chicken or beef bouillon can alternatively be used.

Bring water to a light boil. When the bouillon is dissolved, add tofu squares or noodles.

Simmer tofu for 10 minutes, then turn off stove. Leave tofu in pan, uncovered, until most or all of the liquid is absorbed.

## Cooking Tofu with Taco Seasonings

*Tofu squares cooking in taco-seasoned liquid.*

**INGREDIENTS:**

9 oz. tofu (250 g)
1 tsp. chili mix powder
1 tsp. cumin
½ tsp. salt
¼ tsp. garlic powder
¼ tsp. onion powder
¼ tsp. red pepper flakes
¼ tsp. oregano
¼ tsp. paprika
¼ tsp. pepper
1 Tbsp. tomato paste

Combine all ingredients with 8 ounces of water (236 ml) in pan.

Bring water to a light boil. When the seasonings are dissolved, add tofu squares or noodles.

Simmer tofu for 10 minutes, then turn off stove. Leave tofu in pan, uncovered, until most or all of the liquid is absorbed.

## Cooking Tofu with Curry Seasoning

Tofu squares after cooking and absorbing curry-seasoned liquid.

**INGREDIENTS:**

9 oz. tofu (250 g)
1 tsp. curry powder
1 tsp. vegetable bouillon
½ tsp. salt
¼ tsp. pepper
¼ tsp. red pepper flakes
¼ tsp. cumin
¼ tsp. paprika
¼ tsp. turmeric
¼ tsp. onion powder
¼ tsp. ground ginger
¼ tsp. cinnamon

Combine all ingredients with 8 ounces of water (236 ml) in pan.

Bring water to a light boil. When the seasonings are dissolved, add tofu squares or noodles.

Simmer tofu for 10 minutes, then turn off stove. Leave tofu in pan, uncovered, until most or all of the liquid is absorbed.

## Dehydrating Seasoned Tofu

Place seasoned tofu in a single layer directly on mesh sheets of dehydrator trays.

Dehydrate at 135°F (57°C) for 4–6 hours or until dry and hard.

The smaller the pieces, the faster they dry. Dehydrated tofu is hard. You can snap it in half rather than bend it like jerky. It's too dry to enjoy as a snack, but it rehydrates well in meals.

Tofu noodles on dehydrator tray.

# Recipes with Dehydrated Tofu

## Tofu Noodles with Vegetables & Rice

*Dried tofu noodles, green onion, mushrooms, carrots, and corn.*

*Tofu Noodles with Vegetables & Rice after rehydration.*

**SERVINGS: 1 LARGE**

**INGREDIENTS:**

½ cup dried rice (66 g)
¼ cup dried tofu (20 g)
¼ cup dried spring onions, lightly packed (2 g)
¼ cup dried mushrooms (5 g)
¼ cup dried vegetables (10 g)
1 tsp. vegetable bouillon powder
2 cups water to rehydrate (473 ml)

Add soy sauce to the mushrooms before drying them. This adds flavor to the meal.

Place all dried ingredients in pot with water, and soak 5 minutes. Bring to a boil, and then transfer pot to an insulating cozy for 15 minutes. For thermos preparation, increase water by ¼ cup. Add boiled water to ingredients, and wait 20 minutes, up to several hours.

## Tofu Vegetable Soup

Tofu Vegetable Soup.

**SERVINGS: 1 LARGE**

**INGREDIENTS:**

Same as the previous meal (Tofu Noodles with Vegetables & Rice) without the rice. Dried broccoli substituted for corn.

Water to rehydrate: 2½ cups (591 ml)

Place all dried ingredients in pot with water, and soak 5 minutes. Bring to a boil, and then transfer pot to an insulating cozy for 15 minutes or longer. Use the same amount of boiled water to prepare in a thermos.

## Spicy-Tofu Tortillas

Square-cut taco-flavored tofu after rehydration.

**SERVINGS: 2 TORTILLAS**

**INGREDIENTS:**

½ cup dried taco-spiced tofu squares (45 g)

2 8-inch tortillas

Water to rehydrate: ½ cup (118 ml)

Place dried tofu squares in pot with water. Bring to a boil, and then transfer pot to an insulating cozy for 15 minutes or longer. Spoon rehydrated tofu into tortillas and fold in half. Tip: make 1 at a time, keeping the tofu for the second tortilla warm in the pot. Use same quantity of boiled water to prepare in a thermos.

## Curry Tofu & Vegetables

*Dried curry tofu, apples, carrots, and broccoli.*

*Rehydrated Curry Tofu & Vegetables. Although you can't see it, there is a little curry sauce under the pile that was made with the addition of powdered milk.*

**SERVINGS: 1 LARGE**

**INGREDIENTS:**

½ cup dried curry-seasoned tofu squares or noodles

¼ cup dried carrots (10 g)

¼ cup dried broccoli (5 g)

¼ cup dried apples (10 g)

1¼ cups water to rehydrate (295 ml)

**Optional Ingredients:** 2 Tbsp. powdered milk, or 1 Tbsp. powdered coconut milk.

Place ingredients, except milk or coconut-milk powder, in pot with water, and soak 5 minutes. Bring to a boil, and then transfer pot to an insulating cozy for 15 minutes. Stir in milk powder while there is still a little liquid remaining. Wait another 15 minutes or longer. Increase boiled water by ¼ cup if preparing in a thermos.

# Tofu & Chickpeas Curry Bark

This spicy bark includes tofu, chickpeas, and Indian curry seasonings. It turns into a meal with additional rice and vegetables.

Many curry recipes call for coconut milk to make them silky smooth, but coconut milk will lead to greasy dried meals. With this recipe, the tofu makes a smooth curry sauce without coconut milk.

**INGREDIENTS:**

1 package firm tofu cubes, drained (290 g)

½ can chickpeas, rinsed and drained (125 g)

1 5-oz. can diced tomatoes (400 g), including juice

1 medium red onion, diced (85 g)

2 cloves garlic, minced (12 g)

½ Tbsp. cooking oil

**Indian Curry Spices:**

2 tsp. curry powder

2 tsp. coriander

½ tsp. turmeric

½ tsp. cayenne pepper

1 tsp. ground cumin

1½ tsp. paprika

2 tsp. garam masala

½ tsp. salt

## About Curry Powder

Coriander, turmeric, and cayenne pepper are ingredients found in most curry powders. If you don't have them on hand, you can increase the curry powder accordingly. Garam masala is a blend of Indian spices including coriander, black pepper, cumin, cardamom, and cinnamon. The quantities of spices listed will get you in the ballpark of a tasty curry. Adjust as your senses lead you. Folks who like more heat can add more cayenne pepper or a diced red chili pepper.

## Cooking Tofu & Chickpeas Curry Bark

Cook the onion and garlic for 5 minutes in ½ tablespoon of cooking oil. Add all spices, and cook another 5 minutes. Instead of using more oil, add the juice from the diced tomatoes a little at a time.

Add the tofu, half a can of drained chickpeas, and tomatoes. Bring to a boil, and then simmer on low for 30 minutes.

Allow the mixture to cool, then run it through a blender to a smoothielike consistency. This recipe yields 3 cups after blending.

## Dehydrating Tofu & Chickpeas Curry Bark

Spread thinly on dehydrator trays. If you spread it too thick, it won't rehydrate as well. If using an Excalibur Dehydrator, 1 cup of mixture is a good amount per tray.

Dehydrate at 135°F for 6–8 hours. When done, the bark will be cracked and puffy, like dried mud, and it will crumble easily.

## Rehydrating Tofu & Chickpeas Curry with Rice & Vegetables

**SERVINGS: 1 X-LARGE OR 2 REGULAR**

**INGREDIENTS:**

¾ cup precooked-and-dried rice* (85 g)
⅓ cup curry-bark crumbles (32 g)
⅓ cup dried assorted vegetables** (46 g)
2½ cups water to rehydrate (591 ml)

* The rice was white basmati cooked in salted water and dried. If adding chicken to the recipe, the rice could be cooked in fat-free chicken broth before drying.

** For vegetables, try a medley of dried carrots, red bell pepper, tomatoes, red onions, and chickpeas.

*Rehydrated Tofu & Chickpeas Curry with Rice & Vegetables.*

Place all dried ingredients in pot with water, and soak for 5 minutes. Bring to a boil for 1 minute, and then transfer pot to an insulating cozy for 15 minutes. A little vigorous stirring will break down any bark that remains. For thermos preparation, use the same amount of boiled water, since a 24-ounce thermos will not accommodate any more. Wait 20 minutes, up to 1 hour.

# 4. Beans, Lentils & Quinoa Recipes

## Pressure-Cooking & Dehydrating Beans

Dehydrated canned beans, most of them split open.

Canned beans split open when you dry them. It doesn't matter if you dry them with the liquid from the can or rinsed. Dry 200 red kidney beans from a can, and you'll get 190 busted-open beans. Despite their shoddy appearance, dried canned beans rehydrate well in meals. Using canned beans saves time.

Pressure-cooking beans results in good-looking beans, with far fewer splitting open during dehydration, and they rehydrate well.

Pressure-cooked red kidney beans before drying.

### Soaking Beans before Pressure-Cooking

This soaking method is from the US Dry Bean Council website: Use 5 times as much water as beans. Combine dry beans with unsalted water in a pot, and bring it to a boil for 3 minutes. Remove the pot from the heat, and let it sit for 5 hours. After 5 hours, rinse the beans, cover with fresh water, and refrigerate overnight, or for at least several hours.

Pressure-cooked beans after drying.

### Pressure-Cooking Beans

In the morning, pour off the soaking water, and put the beans in the pressure cooker with enough fresh water to cover. Flavor enhancers, such as a bay leaf, garlic, onion, or bouillon, may be added if desired. Pressure-cook on high setting (15 psi) for 10 minutes, followed by the quick-release method to let out the pressure. Allow beans to cool.

Rehydrated pressure-cooked beans.

### Dehydrating Beans

Dehydrate at 125°F (52°C) for 6–8 hours or until no moisture remains when you open up a few beans. Dry beans on mesh sheets without nonstick sheets.

Experiment Result: Out of 200 beans, 160 beans held together and 40 beans busted open. That's 80 percent intact beans, much better than canned beans. They all rehydrated well when included in meals.

# Rice with Red Beans & Vegetables

*Pressure-cooked-and-dried beans with dried rice and vegetables, after rehydration*

### SERVINGS: 1 LARGE

### INGREDIENTS:

¾ cup dried rice (precooked in vegetable or chicken broth before drying) (100 g)

⅓ cup dried red beans (25 g)

⅓ cup dried mixed vegetables, such as a combination of peas and carrots (25 g)

Salt and pepper to taste

1¾ cups water to rehydrate (414 ml)

**Optional Ingredient:** 2 Tbsp. vegetable-soup powder. Use ¼ cup more water if adding soup powder. *See **Vegetable-Soup Powder**, page 13.*

**Cheese Option:** 2 Tbsp. cheese powder plus 1½ Tbsp. milk powder. Increase water by ½ cup. For cooking in pot, stir in cheese and milk powders after removing pot from stove.

**Pot Cooking:** Soak ingredient for 5 minutes, then bring to a boil for 1 minute. Transfer pot to an insulating cozy for 15 minutes.

**Thermos Cooking:** Use ¼–½ cup more water if making the meal in the morning to eat for lunch. Add boiled water to ingredients in thermos. Wait at least 20 minutes, up to several hours.

# Three Sisters Stew

Early European settlers in the New World learned an Old World agricultural trick from the native inhabitants. Three crops were planted together in a single mound of dirt with a fish head buried in it for fertilizer. Corn was planted in the center of the mound first. When it was 6 inches tall, beans and squash were planted around it. The beans climbed up the corn for support and sunlight. The squash covered the ground and helped to retain soil moisture and suppress weeds.

The three sisters—corn, beans, and squash—are a perfect combination. Not only do beans add nitrogen to soil, which corn and squash need, they also make a "complete" protein for humans when combined with corn, which lacks what beans possess—lysine and tryptophan.

*(Left) Dried Three Sisters Stew ingredients; (right) Three Sisters Stew rehydrated.*

### SERVINGS: 1 LARGE

### INGREDIENTS:

½ cup precooked-and-dried coarse grits (50 g), or ¼ cup uncooked fine grits (45 g)
½ cup dried Zucchini Ratatouille (30 g)*
¼ cup dried beans (20 g)
2 cups water to rehydrate (355 ml)

*See How to Make and Dry Zucchini Ratatouille on next page.*

**Pot Cooking with Precooked-and-Dried Coarse Grits:** Place all ingredients in pot with water, and soak 5 minutes. Bring to a boil for 1 minute. Transfer pot to an insulating cozy for 15 minutes.

**Pot Cooking with Uncooked Fine Grits:** Hold grits back, since fine grits cook almost instantly. Place other ingredients in pot with water, and soak 5 minutes. Bring to a boil, then add grits, and continue cooking a few more seconds. Transfer pot to an insulating cozy for 15 minutes. By adding the grits later in the cooking process, the pot will be easier to clean.

# How to Make and Dry Zucchini Ratatouille

**SERVINGS: 2–4**

**INGREDIENTS:**

½ Tbsp. or less cooking oil
1 small onion, diced
1 large red pepper, diced
1 clove garlic, minced
3 medium zucchinis, sliced and quartered
2 medium tomatoes, diced*
½ tsp. dried basil
½ tsp. herbs de Provence (or Italian-seasoning blend)
¼ tsp. red pepper flakes
Salt and pepper to taste

*A can of diced tomatoes may be used in place of fresh.

Use just enough cooking oil to fry the vegetables on medium heat, starting with the onions for a few minutes. Add the rest of the vegetables one at a time, cooking a few minutes each before adding the next. The best order of adding them is onions, peppers, garlic, and zucchini. Add the herbs when you add the zucchini.

Once the vegetables and herbs are well combined and steaming, add the diced tomatoes. Bring to a light boil, then reduce heat to low, cover, and simmer for 10 minutes. Adjust seasonings and salt and pepper as needed.

## Dehydrating Zucchini Ratatouille

Allow ratatouille to cool, and then spread out on dehydrator trays covered with nonstick sheets. Try to keep any pieces from overlapping each other. Use all juices.

Dehydrate at 135°F (57°C) for 12–14 hours.

Stir ratatouille around 2 or 3 times during the dehydration process to speed up dehydration.

**Dried Yield:** 1 cup dried.

Dried Zucchini Ratatouille can be used in recipes as the vegetable component in combination with choice of starches (grits, pasta, or rice) and proteins (beans, lentils, quinoa, ground beef, chicken, or shrimp).

# Cooking and Dehydrating Quinoa

*Uncooked white quinoa.*

*Quinoa seeds come in several varieties: red, white, black, and tri-color.*

*Cooked red quinoa.*

## Cooking Quinoa

Rinse quinoa several times by pouring water over the seeds in the pot. The seeds sink to the bottom, making it easy to pour off the water. Quinoa has a bitter-tasting coating called saponin, which is mostly removed in commercially available quinoa, but rinse just in case.

Combine 1 cup quinoa with 2 cups liquid, such as bouillon-seasoned water or broth. Plain water may be used. Add ¼ tsp. salt.

Bring to a boil, and then reduce to lowest temperature for about 30 minutes with pot covered.

**Yield:** 1 cup quinoa seeds yields approximately 3 cups of cooked quinoa. Dry weight is approximately 260 grams.

## Dehydrating Quinoa

Spread on dehydrator trays covered with nonstick sheets. If using an Excalibur Dehydrator, 1 cup of cooked quinoa will fit on 1 tray. It will form a mat. Break into smaller pieces when close to dry.

Dehydrate at 135°F (57°C) for 8–10 hours or until crispy.

## Using Dried Quinoa

For backpacking meal variety, use dried quinoa in place of dried rice. Because of its high protein content, it is an excellent choice for meatless entrees.

Quinoa rehydrates well in hot or cold water.

*See recipes for **Inca Stew** on page 46 and **Quinoa & Bean Cilantro Salad** on page 94.*

Dried quinoa can be eaten dry as a crunchy and slightly nutty-tasting ingredient in homemade trail mixes.

# Dehydrating Baked Sweet Potatoes

Poke a few holes in top of medium sweet potatoes with a fork, and use a cookie sheet under the potatoes since some juices will bubble out.

Place sweet potatoes in oven preheated to 375°F (190°C) and bake for 50 minutes or a little longer for larger potatoes.

Remove sweet potatoes from oven, let cool, and remove skins. The skins slip right off.

Slice potatoes crosswise about ⅜- to ½-inch thick (1 cm), and then cut the slices into small cubes of the same thickness. If potatoes have gotten too soft, place in the freezer for a few minutes to firm them up for easier cutting.

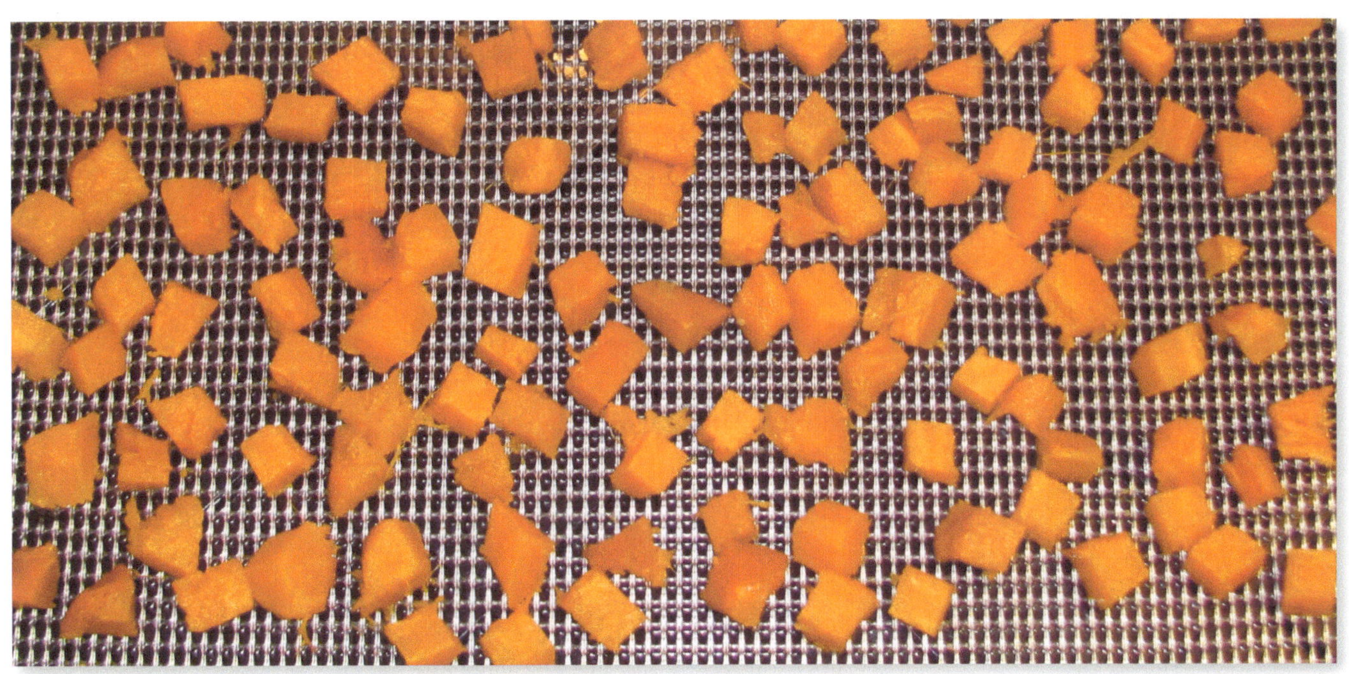

*Baked sweet potatoes cut into cubes on dehydrator tray.*

## Dehydrating Baked Sweet Potatoes

Spread cubed sweet potatoes on dehydrator tray without a nonstick sheet.

Dehydrate at 135°F (57°C) for 10–12 hours.

Dried sweet potato cubes can be eaten dry, but they are a little chewy.

Include a few dried sweet potato cubes as part of the vegetable component in assembled backpacking recipes. They add color and extra nutrition. *See **Inca Stew** on next page.*

# Inca Stew

Machu Picchu, an Inca site situated at 7,970 feet above sea level (2,430 meters), was constructed in the mid-fifteenth century at the height of the Inca Empire.

What kind of food is considered "good eating" at 7,970 feet? For the Inca civilization, 2 important crops were quinoa and sweet potatoes. Those 2 crops were first cultivated several thousand years ago in the Andean region of South America.

Quinoa was a hardy plant that grew well in the mountains where temperatures during the growing season could dip below freezing at night and rise to near 100°F (38°C) during the day. Sweet potatoes grew well at the lower elevations. The harvested quinoa seeds and sweet potatoes stored well, providing a secure and reliable food source that enabled the Inca Empire to thrive until the Spanish Conquest in the mid-sixteenth century.

Quinoa and sweet potatoes are very nutritious. The edible seeds of the quinoa plant are high in protein, fiber, phosphorus, magnesium, iron, and calcium. Sweet potatoes are high in complex carbohydrates, fiber, beta-carotene (vitamin A), vitamin C, calcium, folate, and potassium. Sweet potatoes also contain antioxidant and anti-inflammatory nutrients.

With all of these health benefits, quinoa and sweet potatoes top the list of backpacking superfoods, so we put them together for a tasty Inca Stew.

Rehydrated Inca Stew.

*Dried ingredients for 1 serving of Inca Stew: quinoa, ratatouille, and sweet potatoes.*

**SERVINGS: 1 LARGE**

**INGREDIENTS:**

½ cup precooked-and-dried quinoa (45 g)

½ cup dried vegetables, any kind (40 g)

¼ cup precooked-and-dried diced sweet potatoes (20 g)

1¼ cups water to rehydrate (295 ml)

Notes: Since these food ingredients can stand on their own, it's not necessary to add any special seasonings other than cooking the quinoa with an all-natural bouillon cube and cooking the vegetables with a pinch of Italian herbs and salt and pepper.

For vegetables, a simple dried ratatouille (zucchini, red bell pepper, onion, tomato, and garlic) works well, but any combination of dried vegetables is fine.

Drying quinoa separately allows you to use it in other recipes as an alternative to rice. Quinoa behaves just like precooked-and-dried rice in backpacking meals and rehydrates well.

*See **Dehydrating Quinoa** on page 44, and **Dehydrating Baked Sweet Potatoes** on page 45.*

**Pot Cooking:** Combine ingredients in pot with water. Soak 5 minutes and bring to a boil for 1 minute. Transfer pot to an insulating cozy for 15 minutes.

**Thermos Cooking:** Add an extra ¼ cup boiled water (1½ cups) to ingredients in a thermos food jar. Wait 20 minutes, up to several hours.

# Green-Lentil Chili

**SERVINGS: 4**

**INGREDIENTS:**

1½ cups green lentils (300g)
1 15-oz. can diced tomatoes (400 g)
1 15-oz. can kidney beans (400 g)
2 medium onions, diced (130 g)
½ Tbsp. cooking oil
2–3 cloves garlic, minced
3 Tbsp. tomato paste
3 Tbsp. chili mix powder
1½ tsp. salt
1 tsp. ground cumin
¼ tsp. pepper
½ tsp. oregano
2 bay leaves
3 Tbsp. brewed coffee (optional)
3 Tbsp. apple-cider vinegar

**Dehydrate Separately:**
6–8 carrots
3–4 bell peppers

## Cooking Green-Lentil Chili

Green lentils were used for this recipes because they stay firm when cooked. Red lentils tend to get mushy.

Rinse lentils first to remove any dust or debris.

In a stockpot, bring lentils to a boil in 4 cups of water or bullion (800 ml) seasoned with bay leaves and ground cumin. Do not add salt yet, as salt on the front end makes lentils tougher. Reduce heat, and simmer for 30 minutes.

When the lentils are almost done, start cooking the other ingredients in a separate pan.

Coat pan with minimal cooking oil, and cook onions and garlic for 5 minutes on medium heat.

Add all the dry seasonings and the tomato paste. Continue stirring a few more minutes.

Add the cooked lentils, rinsed kidney beans, diced tomatoes, and brewed coffee (optional) to the pan. Increase heat until bubbling, and then reduce to a low simmer for 30 minutes.

Adjust seasonings to taste during the last 5 minutes of cooking. Remove chili from stove and stir in the apple-cider vinegar. Balsamic vinegar may be used in place of apple-cider vinegar.

*Rehydrated Green-Lentil Chili.*

## Dehydrating Green-Lentil Chili

Dehydrate at 135°F (57°C) for 8–10 hours or until crispy.

This recipe makes 6 cups of chili (wet). If using an Excalibur Dehydrator, 2 cups of chili will fit nicely on each of 3 trays covered with nonstick sheets.

*1 serving of dried Green Lentil Chili and Vegetables.*

## Dehydrating Extra Vegetables

Carrots and bell peppers can be cooked in the chili, but they tend to lose some color and texture when stewed. To achieve better color and texture, dry them separately, and add them to the meal later.

Steam carrots for 6 minutes before drying them. They will turn dark orange and hold their color better than if dried raw. Bell peppers can be dried raw. Dehydrate at the same time as the chili.

**SERVINGS: 1 LARGE**

1 cup Green-Lentil Chili (112 g)
¼ cup dried vegetables (20 g)
1¾ cups water to rehydrate (414 ml)

**Pot Cooking:** Combine chili and vegetables in pot with water. If you like your chili saucy, add a bit more water. Soak 5 minutes, and bring to a boil for 1 minute. Transfer pot to an insulating cozy for 15 minutes.

**Thermos Cooking:** Use an extra ¼ cup of water. Add 2 cups of boiled water (473 ml) to ingredients in a thermos food jar. Wait 20 minutes, up to several hours.

# Red-Lentil Curry

Red lentils turn mushy when you cook them, unlike green lentils, which stay firm. To turn red lentils into a flavorful sauce, run the cooked red-lentil curry through a blender, and then dry it into bark. Assemble meals using the bark, dried brown-basmati rice, and colorful dried vegetables.

**INGREDIENTS:**

2 tsp. cooking oil
1 medium onion, diced
1 clove garlic, minced
1 Tbsp. ginger, grated
3 Tbsp. curry powder*
1 Tbsp. cumin seeds
2 cups red lentils
6 cups water (1.4 L)
1 tsp. salt

*Curry powder used was a blend of coriander, turmeric, yellow mustard, fenugreek, cumin, ginger, pepper, onion, garlic, bay leaves, paprika, cayenne pepper, and nutmeg.

Cumin seeds and fresh ginger give the curry a little extra zing.

## How to make Red-Lentil Curry Bark

Begin by lubricating a stockpot with 2 teaspoons of cooking oil. Cook the onions, garlic, and grated ginger over medium heat for a few minutes.

Add the curry powder and cumin seeds. Stir to toast the spices a little.

Add a few ounces of water at a time, cooking the mixture down to a pastelike consistency before adding a little more water. After 15 minutes or so, the flavor of the spices will have blossomed.

Add the lentils and rest of the water. Bring to a boil, then reduce the heat to low, and simmer for 15 minutes. Stir in 1 teaspoon of salt at the end. Remove pot from heat and let cool.

## Dehydrating Red-Lentil-Curry Bark

Run the cooked red lentils through a blender until smooth, or use an immersion blender. The yield from this recipe is approximately 5 cups of blended lentils. You will be able to make several trail meals from this quantity.

Spread blended lentils evenly on dehydrator trays covered with nonstick sheets. In an Excalibur Dehydrator, 2 cups of lentils fit on 1 tray.

Dehydrate at 135°F (57°C) for 8–10 hours or until dry and crumbly.

**Yield:** 5 cups of blended mixture yields 3¾ cups crumbled bark (450 g).

## Cooking and Dehydrating Brown-Basmati Rice

Cook rice on a back burner while making the red-lentil curry. Rinse brown rice before cooking.

Combine 2 cups of brown-basmati rice (400 g) with 2 cups water (473 ml) and 1 teaspoon salt. Bring to a boil, reduce heat to low, and simmer for 45 minutes. Keep lid on pot while the rice is simmering, no stirring. Remove from heat, and let sit until cool. Note: If you use white rice instead of brown rice, you will use more water, and the cooking time will be shorter.

**Dehydrating Rice:** 2 cups of brown-basmati rice will yield 5 cups of cooked rice. Spread the cooked rice on dehydrator trays covered with nonstick sheets and dehydrate at 135°F (57°C) for 6–8 hours or until dry and hard. If dried in the same load as the bark, it will probably finish drying before the bark. A single Excalibur Dehydrator tray will hold 2½ to 3 cups of cooked rice. After the brown-basmati rice is dried, you will again end up with approximately 2 cups. It will rehydrate and cook quickly in trail meals.

*Red-Lentil Curry with Brown-Basmati Rice & Vegetables, dried and rehydrated.*

## Red-Lentil Curry with Brown-Basmati Rice & Vegetables

**1 Regular Serving:** ¼ cup red-lentil-curry bark (30 g), ½ cup dried brown-basmati rice (67 g), ½ cup dried vegetables (40 g), 1¼ cups water to rehydrate (295 ml).

**1 Large Serving:** ⅓ cup red-lentil-curry bark (40 g), ¾ cup dried brown-basmati rice (100 g), ¾ cup dried vegetables (60 g), 1¾ cups water to rehydrate (414 ml).

**Vegetables:** Use a colorful medley of dried vegetables, such as carrots, red bell peppers, red serrano peppers, and baked sweet potato.

**Pot Cooking:** Combine all ingredients in pot with water. Soak 5 minutes, and bring to a boil for 1 minute. Transfer pot to an insulating cozy for 15 minutes.

**Thermos Cooking:** Use an extra ¼–⅓ cup water, depending on the serving size. Add boiled water to ingredients in thermos food jar, and wait 20 minutes, up to several hours.

# Green-Lentil Stew

**SERVINGS: 4**

**INGREDIENTS:**

1 onion, diced
2 cups leeks, chopped
1–2 carrots, diced
1 tomato, diced
1 red bell pepper, diced
1 clove garlic, minced
1 bay leaf
½ lb. mushrooms, sliced (250 g)
1⅔ cups green lentils (300 g)
2½ cups vegetable broth (591 ml)
Handful chopped parsley
1 Tbsp. cooking oil
2 tsp. balsamic vinegar
Salt and pepper to taste

## Cooking Green-Lentil Stew

Lubricate a stockpot with ½ tablespoon of cooking oil. Cook onions, leeks, and garlic for 10 minutes on medium heat. Add carrots, tomatoes, and bell peppers, and continue cooking a few more minutes. Hold back the mushrooms and parsley.

Add lentils, and cook another 5 minutes.

Add vegetable broth, and bring to a boil. Reduce heat to low, and simmer for 30 minutes, covered.

In a separate, minimally lubricated pan, cook sliced mushrooms and chopped parsley. Add 2 teaspoons of balsamic vinegar or a splash of wine if desired.

Add cooked mushrooms to cooked lentils in stockpot, and simmer another 5 minutes. Remove from stove, and allow to cool for dehydration.

## Dehydrating Green-Lentil Stew

Spread stew on dehydrator trays covered with nonstick sheets. For this recipe, 3 Excalibur Dehydrator trays were used.

Dehydrate at 135°F (57°C) for 10–12 hours or until all components of the stew are dry. Check the mushrooms to make sure they are dry on the inside

## Rehydrating Green-Lentil Stew

*(Left) Dehydrated Green-Lentil Stew. (Right) Rehydrated Green-Lentil Stew.*

**1 Regular Serving:** ¾ cup dried stew, 1 cup water to rehydrate or a little more.

**1 Large Serving:** 1 cup dried stew, 1⅓ cup water to rehydrate or a little more.

A little extra water is fine with this meal, as it creates a gravy. Rehydrated green lentils remain firm and chewy.

**Pot Cooking:** Combine all ingredients in pot with water. Soak 5 minutes, and bring to a boil for 1 minute. Transfer pot to an insulating cozy for 15 minutes.

**Thermos Cooking:** Use an extra ¼–⅓ cup water, depending on the serving size. Add boiled water to ingredients in thermos food jar, and wait 20 minutes, up to several hours.

**A note on color:** The green (more like brown) of lentils, and the stew-making process in general, deplete the color of the carrots and red bell pepper. For a more colorful meal, dehydrate additional vegetables separately, and add them to the dried meal when rehydrating. A few more carrots, yellow bell peppers, or cubes of sweet potatoes will brighten up the stew. If adding an extra ¼ cup of dried vegetables, increase water for rehydration by ¼ cup.

# 5. Beef, Poultry, Seafood & Ham

## Meatloaf

**MEATLOAF INGREDIENTS:**

1 pound of ground beef (454 g)
1 cup of shredded bread
1 grated carrot
1 diced onion
1 minced garlic clove
1 egg

Use lean ground beef if you plan to dehydrate it. You can make a bigger loaf with 1½ pounds of ground beef and a little more of the other ingredients. Stick with 1 egg unless you're making a 2-pound loaf.

Mush it all together, and form it into a loaf.

**Meatloaf Sauce Ingredients:**

2 Tbsp. ketchup
1 tsp. spicy mustard
1 tsp. brown sugar
½ tsp. Worcestershire sauce.

Put the loaf on top of baking paper in a loaf pan. Coat the top with half the sauce. Place in oven preheated to 400°F (200°C). Bake 45–55 minutes, adding the rest of the sauce near the end.

Check that the meatloaf is cooked just right by inserting a meat thermometer into the center. It should be 160°F (70°C) when done.

## Dehydrating Meatloaf

Remove the loaf from the pan as soon as it is done, and separate it from the parchment paper. Place it momentarily on several layers of paper towels to absorb any grease.

Once the meatloaf has cooled, slice and dice it into ½-inch cubes.

Spread meatloaf cubes out on dehydrator tray covered with a nonstick sheet.

Dehydrate at 145°F (63°C) for 8–10 hours or until dry.

## Meatloaf with Noodles and Green Beans

*Dried noodles, meatloaf, and green beans.*

**Servings:** 1 Large

**Dried Ingredients:** 1 cup meatloaf (75 g), ¾ cup noodles (50 g), and ⅓ cup green beans (13 g).

**Pot Cooking:** Soak the ingredients in 1¾ cups of water (414 ml) for 5 minutes, bring to a boil for 1 minute, then transfer the pot to an insulating cozy, and wait 15 to 20 minutes.

**Thermos Cooking:** Add 2¼ cups of boiled water (532 ml) to the ingredients in the thermos food jar, and enjoy 30 minutes or up to several hours later.

# Meatballs

Meatloaf and meatballs are pretty much the same thing. For this recipe, start out cooking a "Meatball Loaf" with extra garlic, Italian herbs, and plenty of marinara sauce.

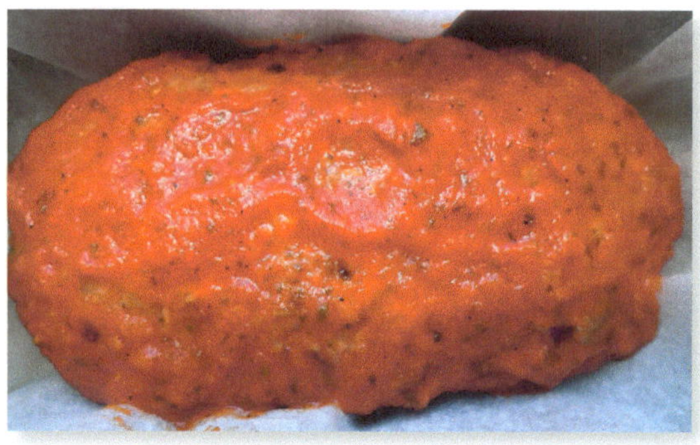

**MEATBALL INGREDIENTS:**

1 lb. lean ground beef (454 g)
1 egg
1 cup bread, shredded
1 large carrot, grated
1 medium onion, diced
2 cloves garlic, minced
1 tsp. Italian herbs*
¼ tsp. crushed red pepper
1 cup marinara sauce (237 ml)

*For herbs, try a generous pinch each of dried basil, oregano, and herbs de Provence.

## Cooking the Meatball Loaf

Combine all ingredients in a bowl, and mix well with hands. Form into a loaf. It's easier to cut the cooked meat later into uniform pieces if the meat is cooked as a loaf rather than as meatballs.

Place loaf in a loaf pan lined with parchment paper. Coat the top of the loaf with some of the marinara sauce, and set aside the rest until after the loaf is cooked.

Bake in preheated oven at 400°F (200°C) for 45 to 55 minutes. Internal temperature should be 160°F (70°C) when the loaf is done.

When fully cooked, remove loaf from pan, and separate from parchment paper. Place it momentarily on several layers of paper towels to absorb any grease.

## Dehydrating the Meatball Loaf

Once loaf has cooled, cut it into ½-inch cubes, and coat thoroughly with remaining sauce.

Spread coated meat out in a single layer on dehydrator trays covered with nonstick sheets.

Dehydrate at 145°F (63°C) for 8–10 hours or until no moisture remains.

## Meatball Sandwich

A meatball sandwich makes an excellent hot lunch, prepared in advance. If using a thermos food jar, add boiled water to the dried meat and spinach in the thermos, and wait 30 minutes up to several hours.

A 24-ounce capacity thermos food jar will hold double the recipe, so you can enjoy two meatball sandwiches, or share one with a partner.

After rehydrating the meat in hot water, ¼ cup of tasty juice will remain, which tastes amazingly good as it soaks into the bread. Bread won't keep long in a backpack, so plan this meal for the first or second day of a trip.

You can also make a traditional pasta meal with meatballs.

**SERVINGS: 1 LARGE**

1 cup dried meatballs (75 g)

¼ cup dried spinach (3 g)

1 ciabatta roll, or similarly stout bread

1¼ cups water to rehydrate (295 ml)

Add salt and pepper to taste when serving.

## Meatballs with Pasta & Spinach

**Pot Cooking:** Soak ingredients in pot for 5 minutes, bring to a boil for 1 minute, then transfer the pot to an insulating cozy for 15 minutes.

**Thermos Cooking:** Use an extra ¼ cup water. Add boiled water to ingredients in thermos. If you plan to eat several hours later, consider adding the pasta 30 minutes before you eat. This will ensure firm pasta with a good bite.

As with the meatball sandwich, there will be a ¼ cup of tasty marina-beef juices remaining, which enhances the meal.

**SERVINGS: 1 LARGE**

¾ cup dried meatballs (55 g)

¾ cup dried pasta (34 g)

¼ cup dried spinach (3 g)

1¾ cups water to rehydrate (414 ml)

Salt and pepper to taste when serving. Parmesan cheese is nice on top.

To increase this meal's sauciness, add a ¼ cup of marinara-sauce leather. Keep the water the same or increase it slightly when rehydrating and cooking the meal on the trail.

# Dehydrating Ground Beef with Seasonings

When breadcrumbs are added to ground beef, it rehydrates much better than ground beef dried without a starch. People often ask, "Is there a gluten-free alternative to using breadcrumbs?"

The good news is yes. Ground rolled oats or millet also provide excellent results.

While neither oats nor millet contain gluten, they may be processed in a facility that processes other grains that do contain gluten. Look for gluten-free certification on the label if you're in the highly sensitive category.

Breadcrumbs or ground oats, and seasonings, can also be used to improve rehydration when cooking and dehydrating ground chicken and turkey.

## Seasoning Ground Beef

Use only lean ground beef with fat content in the 7 to 10 percent range.

Grind rolled oats or millet flakes into flour in a blender, or use fine breadcrumbs. Use ½ cup of ground oats or breadcrumbs per pound of ground beef. Add seasonings as desired.

**Basic Seasonings for 1 pound of lean ground beef (454 g):**

½ cup fine breadcrumbs or ground oats, ½ teaspoon each of salt, garlic powder, onion powder, chili powder, and cumin. For a hotter and spicier blend, try breakfast-sausage seasonings.

**Breakfast-Sausage Seasonings for 1 pound of lean ground beef (454 g):**

**INGREDIENTS:**

½ cup fine breadcrumbs or ground oats
1 tsp. brown sugar
1 tsp. salt
1 tsp. pepper
½ tsp. onion powder
1 tsp. dried sage
1 tsp. dried basil
¼ tsp. dried marjoram
⅛ tsp. red pepper flakes

Add ½ tsp. cayenne pepper for more heat.

Add 1 tsp. Worcestershire sauce or soy sauce to the beef, if desired.

## Cooking Ground Beef

Sprinkle seasoned breadcrumbs/ground oats evenly over ground beef, and slowly work it into the beef. Form the ground beef into a big meatball and set aside for a few minutes.

Pull the seasoned ground beef apart into small pieces. The meat is easier to cook evenly in ½-pound batches.

Place meat in a cold, nonstick pan. Begin heating pan on medium. This allows the meat to sweat out a tiny amount of grease so you don't need to oil the pan.

Increase the heat to medium high, and continue cooking (about 10 minutes; lots of stirring) until the meat is lightly browned and cooked through.

## Dehydrating Ground Beef

Place cooked ground beef in a single layer on dehydrator tray. Note in the photo that the nonstick sheet is under, rather than over, the mesh sheet. This allows for greater air circulation around the meat. You still need the nonstick sheet to catch any small bits of meat.

Dehydrate at 145°F (63°C) for 4–6 hours. Since the meat is precooked, there is no need to dry it at a higher temperature.

## Rehydrating Dried Ground Beef

Dehydrated ground beef, enhanced with breadcrumbs, ground oats, or ground millet, rehydrates quickly with hot water. Use a 1:1 ratio of water to ground beef. So, for ⅓ cup of dried ground beef, use ⅓ cup of water. If eyeballing it, add just enough water to cover the meat.

Heat to a light boil in pot, then set pot aside for a few minutes until meat absorbs all the water.

When including dried ground beef in a quick-cooking meal of grits or couscous, soak and heat the ground beef with enough water for the complete meal before adding the grits or couscous. For most other meals, the dried meat and ingredients can be cooked at the same time.

# Dehydrating Ground Chicken and Turkey

Can ground chicken and turkey be dehydrated the same way as ground beef? Specifically, does the breadcrumb trick work equally well for poultry?

The answer is yes; adding breadcrumbs to ground poultry before you cook and dehydrate it results in meat that rehydrates well in meals. The meat retains a pleasant chewiness; you won't have to suffer through extremely tough meat like you will if the breadcrumbs are left out.

Ground oats may be used in place of breadcrumbs as a gluten-free option. Grind rolled oats into flour and use the same quantity as breadcrumbs (½ cup per pound of ground meat).

Some folks dehydrate meat raw. They add seasonings and lots of sodium, squeeze the ground meat through a jerky gun onto dehydrator trays, and then dry it at 165°F (74°C). While this is a time-honored method, there remains the possibility that pathogens in the meat may survive the dehydration process, especially if the dehydrator doesn't run as hot as advertised.

Poultry meat has a looser cellular structure than beef, so there are more spaces for pathogens to hang out in. For that reason, cook it twice: first on the stove and then in the oven.

## Cooking Ground Chicken and Turkey

As with ground beef, use only low-fat ground poultry.

For each pound of ground poultry (454 g), add ½ cup fine breadcrumbs or ground oats. Gluten-free bread or cracker crumbs may also be used. Season the breadcrumbs or oats as desired.

Work breadcrumbs into meat a little at a time with your fingers. Form the meat into a ball, set aside for a few minutes, and then pull the meat apart into small pieces. This can be a sticky affair.

Before cooking the meat on the stove, preheat oven to 350°F (180°C).

Lightly oil a nonstick pan with 1 teaspoon of cooking oil. Add all meat at the same time, and fry on medium high for 5 to 6 minutes, until the meat is no longer pink. Stir and flip meat continuously with spatula, chopping any larger pieces in half. Some of the meat will brown lightly, which is a desirable trait.

Transfer fried ground meat to a glass or ceramic baking dish, and place in preheated oven at 350°F (180°C) for 10 minutes.

After 10 minutes, turn off oven, but leave meat in there for another 10 minutes. Don't let any heat out by opening the oven door. After a total of 20 minutes in the oven, remove meat, and let it cool.

## Dehydrating Ground Chicken and Turkey

Once cool enough to handle, spread the cooked meat out in a single layer on dehydrator trays. Tear any larger pieces into smaller pieces.

Dehydrate at 145°F (63°C) for 6–8 hours or until no moisture remains when you break any pieces in half.

Since the meat has been thoroughly cooked at a high temperature, there is no need to dehydrate at 165°F (74°C).

*Ground chicken (left) and ground turkey (right) after drying.*

The mesh sheets are on top of rather than under the nonstick sheets. This improves air circulation around the meat, while the nonstick sheets catch any small bits of dried meat that fall through.

# Turkey with Rice & Vegetables

This simple meal lets the flavor of the individual foods stand on their own rather than be covered up with sauces. Add variety to your backpacking menus by substituting ground chicken or turkey for ground beef. The ground poultry will be tenderer than dried whole chicken meat. Pressure-cooked poultry can be used too.

*Dried ingredients in Turkey with Rice & Vegetables.*

**SERVINGS: 1 LARGE**

**INGREDIENTS:**

¾ cup precooked-and-dried rice* (100 g)

⅓ cup dried ground turkey or chicken (40 g)

⅓ cup dried mixed vegetables (25 g), green beans and carrots shown above

1½ cups water to rehydrate (355 ml)

*Rice precooked in chicken broth will add more chicken flavor to the meal.

**Pot Cooking:** Combine dried ingredients with 1½ cups water (355 ml) in pot, and soak for 5 minutes. Bring to boil, and continue cooking for 1 minute. Transfer pot to an insulating cozy for 15 minutes.

**Thermos Cooking:** Use ¼ cup more water. Add 1¾ cups boiled water (414 ml) to dried ingredients in thermos food jar. Wait 20 minutes, up to several hours.

*Rehydrated Turkey with Rice & Vegetables.*

# Pressure-Cooking and Dehydrating Chicken

Pressure-cooking chicken infuses the chicken with aromatic seasonings while retaining all the flavor of the chicken itself. After a few minutes in the pressure cooker, the chicken will be fully cooked, tender, and delicious. As a bonus, you end up with rich-tasting chicken stock to be used in the dehydration process. Breast meat is low in fat, which makes it better for storage than the fattier thighs and legs.

*Pressure-cooked chicken before drying.*

After you dehydrate chicken, it does not completely rehydrate back to the tender condition it was in before you dried it. Pressure-cooked-and-dried chicken will be chewy, comparable to dried canned chicken, but much easier to chew than dried chicken that was grilled, fried, or baked. It is a little chewier than dehydrated ground chicken that has been precooked with breadcrumbs or ground oats.

## Pressure-Cooking 1 Pound of Chicken Breast Meat

**Start by pressure-cooking a potato in chicken broth.**

When high-protein meat is dehydrated, the cells lock up and don't take back much water when you rehydrate them in a meal. Incorporating a starch into the protein helps the meat rehydrate much better.

- Peel and cut a small potato into cubes, approximately 4 ounces (113 g).
- Put cubes in pressure cooker with 1¼ cups fat-free chicken broth or water with bouillon (300 ml).
- Add ½ tsp. salt.
- Heat until the salt (and bouillon, if added) dissolves. Put lid on pressure cooker.
- Pressure-cook on high for 3 minutes and set aside, allowing the pressure to release on its own rather than using a fast-release method.
- When the potato in the pressure cooker has cooled, mash the potato with a potato masher, including all the liquid in the pot.

Most pressure cookers have 2 pressure settings, low and high, indicated by red lines on the gauge at the top of the pot. The first line pops up at low pressure and the second when high pressure is reached.

Both the potato and the chicken are pressure-cooked using high pressure.

## Cutting and Tenderizing Chicken

Cut chicken breast meat crosswise into strips. This opens up more surface area for tenderizing and infusion of starch and flavors.

Tenderizing breaks down some of the cell walls in the protein, which improves its ability to reabsorb water in a dehydrated meal.

Place chicken pieces between parchment paper and bang on them with a tenderizing mallet, or hammer, as shown. Go ahead…get out some of those aggressions. It will look like your hammer is going right through the meat, but it will still hold together while being thinner when you are done.

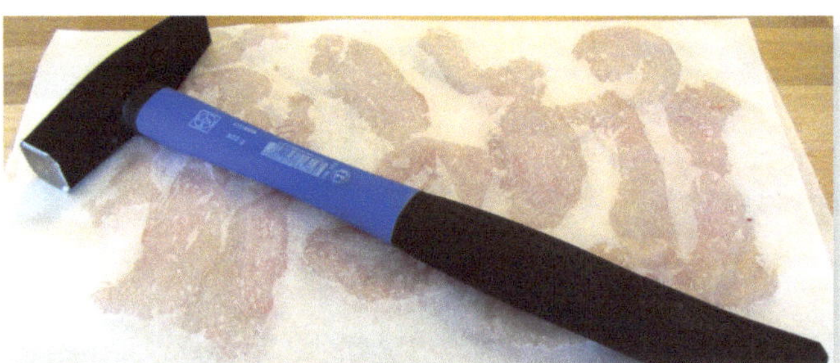

*"Hammered" chicken.*

## Pressure-Cooking Chicken

**INGREDIENTS:**

1 pound or more of chicken breast meat (approximately 500 g)

1 small potato (approximately 4 oz., or 113 g)

1¼ cups fat-free chicken broth or water with bouillon (300 ml)

½ tsp. salt

1 onion slice, separated into rings

1 clove garlic, cut into pieces

1 lemon slice, cut into 4 pieces and squeezed

Fresh herbs: Try 2 sprigs each of rosemary, basil, and parsley. Dried herbs can be used instead.

After preparing the potato broth and hammering the chicken as described, add the rest of the ingredients to the pressure cooker and stir, pushing the herbs down into the liquid and distributing the lemon juice.

Pressure-cook for 10 minutes once high pressure is reached.

Set pot aside and allow pressure to release on its own rather than using a quick pressure release. It will take about 10 minutes for the pressure to release.

*Aromatic ingredients in the pressure cooker with chicken and potato-thickened liquid.*

## Dehydrating Pressure-Cooked Chicken

Remove meat from pressure cooker with tongs, and pull apart into smaller pieces with fingers. Remove any ingredients that may have merged with the meat, but it doesn't hurt to leave a few bits of the herbs.

Spread meat out on dehydrator tray covered with nonstick sheet.

Spoon some of the flavorful liquid from the pressure cooker over the meat on the tray.

Dehydrate at 145°F (63°C) for 4–6 hours or until completely dry. Stir meat around once or twice during dehydration. Dried meat will be crispy.

*Pressure-cooked chicken shown on Excalibur Dehydrator tray.*

*Dried pressure-cooked chicken. Use in meals, or eat it dry as crunchy chicken jerky.*

# Dehydrating Shrimp

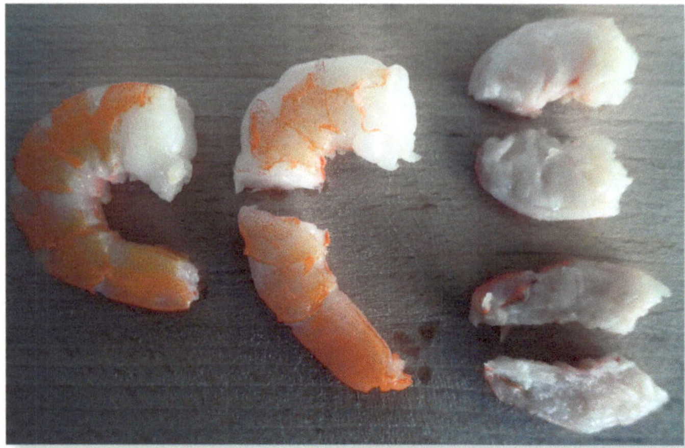

## Cutting and Seasoning Shrimp

**Product:** One pound of frozen, precooked medium peel-and-eat shrimp (454 g).

Cut thawed shrimp in halves and then rotate and cut the halves again down the vein channel. This will maximize the surface area to come in contact with the seasoning.

In a bowl, stir 1 teaspoon of Old Bay Seasoning (or similar seafood seasoning) into cut shrimp. Old Bay Seasoning includes celery salt, red and black pepper, and paprika. Add a few shakes of garlic powder if you like. Set seasoned shrimp aside for a few minutes to let flavors mingle.

Dehydrate shrimp at 145°F (63°C) for 5–6 hours or until hard. Break a piece in half, and check to make sure there is no moisture inside.

## Hawaiian Shrimp & Rice

**Large Serving:** ¾ cup dried rice (100 g), ⅓ cup dried mixed vegetables (25 g), 3 Tbsp. dried pineapple (10 g), and ⅓ cup dried shrimp (25 g). Rehydrate and cook with 1½–1¾ cups water (355–414 ml).

## Shrimp Linguine

**SERVINGS: 1 LARGE**

**INGREDIENTS:**

¾ cup dried linguine (70 g)

⅓ cup dried shrimp (25 g)

⅓ cup dried mixed vegetables (25 g), peppers, tomatoes, mushrooms, and onions shown

⅓ cup dried marinara-sauce leather (25 g)

Pack dried ingredients in a Ziploc bag, but pack marinara-sauce leather in its own smaller bag. Consider optional packets of parmesan cheese and olive oil.

**Pot Cooking:** Place dried ingredients in pot with 1½ cups water (355 ml). Soak for 5 minutes, then bring to a boil for 1 minute. Transfer pot to an insulating cozy for 15 minutes. Add parmesan cheese and olive oil (optional) after meal is rehydrated.

**Thermos Cooking:** Place dried ingredients in 24-ounce capacity thermos food jar with 1¾ cups of boiled water (414 ml). Wait 20 minutes, up to several hours.

## Dehydrating Linguine

Bring 4 quarts of water (1 L) to a boil with 1 teaspoon of salt. Add 1 16-oz. package of linguine (500 g). Break it into quarters before cooking.

Cook for 6–8 minutes, maintaining a gentle boil. You want it slightly undercooked for dehydrating, since it will get additional cooking on the trail.

*Cooked linguine lightly coated with sauce before drying.*

Drain, and then stir in just enough marinara sauce to coat. This keeps the linguine from sticking together.

Dehydrate at 125°F (52°C) for 5–6 hours or until crispy.

Pull linguine apart a few times while it is drying. It shrinks as it dries.

Drying linguine with a minimal amount of sauce makes the drying go faster and ensures that the pasta dries without any hidden moisture.

When using linguine in Italian-style meals, include additional dried marinara-sauce leather or powdered tomato sauce with the meals. The light coating on the dried linguine is not enough to make a sauce.

# Dehydrating Surimi

Surimi, which resembles the meat of snow crab legs, is a processed food which contains fish and flavors of crustaceans, as well as starches and coloring. You can find it in various shapes and marketed as "artificial crabmeat" or "seafood sticks."

Dehydrated surimi rehydrates well in hot or cold water. *See the **Sushi Rice Salad** recipe, page 98.*

Slice seafood sticks crosswise into ¼ inch thick pieces, and place them on mesh dehydrator tray in a single layer.

Dehydrate at 145°F (63°C) for 5–6 hours until hard.

**Yield:** A 235 gram package of surimi (8.3 oz.) will yield ¾ cup of dried surimi (69 g).

*Dried surimi.*

# Dehydrating Canadian Bacon

Americans call it "Canadian bacon," but Canadians call it "back bacon." Most people agree this lean cut of pork from the loin tastes like ham. With a fat content of only 4 percent, it is a good choice for dehydrating. Canadian bacon is cured, smoked, and fully cooked. It is typically sold in thick slices, round or oblong in shape.

Because it is thick sliced, it is quite chewy if dried in strips. Another way to dry it is to shred it. When dried, the shredded ham resembles bacon bits.

Trim off the hardened outer layer, which will contain some fat. Dice the ham, and then press down hard on the pieces with a kitchen mallet. Pull the mashed ham apart into smaller shreds.

Spread in a single layer on dehydrator trays covered with nonstick sheets.

Dehydrate at 145°F (63°C) for 6–8 hours or until crispy.

Canadian bacon bits can be used in recipes in place of thin-sliced deli ham. They go great with grits, macaroni, couscous, rice, barley, and potatoes. You don't need a lot because they are very flavorful and salty.

**Dry weights:** ¼ cup dried = 25 g; ⅓ cup dried = 33 g

## Grated Potatoes with Vegetables and Canadian Bacon Bits

**INGREDIENTS FOR 1 LARGE SERVING:**

¾ cup dried grated potatoes (48 g)
⅓ cup dried mixed vegetables (25 g)
¼ cup dried Canadian bacon bits (25 g)
Salt and pepper to taste
1¾ cups water to rehydrate (414 ml)

Add slices of cheddar cheese or powdered parmesan cheese after meal is cooked.

# 6. Potato Recipes

## How to Make Instant Potato Powder

Potato bark can cause vacuum-sealed bags to lose their seals due to the bark's sharp edges. It can also require a fair amount of spirited stirring to get it to fully turn back into creamy potatoes in a rehydrated meal. Grinding potato bark into powder solves both of those concerns.

The usual method of making potato bark is to boil potatoes in water, drain them, and then run them through a blender with vegetable, chicken, or beef broth. That method still works fine, but you can also hand mash the potatoes without using a blender.

Another variation, described below, is to boil the potatoes in a smaller amount of seasoned water, and then mash them without draining off any of the liquid.

### Cooking Mashed Potatoes

Boil 2¾ pounds of chunked potatoes (1.25 kg) in 2¾ cups of water (650 ml) seasoned with 1 tablespoon of vegetable bouillon (15 g). Cook until potatoes are soft, about 15 minutes. Mash boiled potatoes with a hand masher, including all the liquid in the pot. Alternatively, you can run them through a blender.

**Yield:** 2¾ pounds of potatoes makes approximately 6¾ cups mashed. If using an Excalibur Dehydrator, spread 1⅓ cups on 5 trays.

### Dehydrating Mashed Potatoes

*1⅓ cups of mashed potatoes spread thinly on dehydrator tray and dried.*

Dehydrate at 135°F (57°C) for 8–10 hours or until brittle.

Once the bark has dried most of the way on nonstick sheets, flip it over directly onto mesh sheets and peel away the nonstick sheets. This helps the bottom side catch up with the top.

Break the dried potato bark into smaller pieces and run it through a blender. Take your time. Lesser quality blenders might overheat if you run them too long.

**Total Yield:** 2¾ pounds of potatoes yields approximately 1¼ cups of potato powder (254 g).

## Potato Bark to Powder Conversions:

A ½ cup portion of potato bark yields 2 tablespoons, plus 2 teaspoons of potato powder, 32 grams total.

A ¾ cup portion of potato bark (shown above) yields 4 tablespoons of potato powder, 48 grams total.

## Creamy Potatoes with Ground Beef & Vegetables

**SERVINGS: 1 LARGE**

**INGREDIENTS:**

4 Tbsp. potato powder (48 g), equivalent to ¾ cup bark

⅓ cup dried ground beef (35 g)

⅓ cup dried vegetables (25 g)

1¾ cups water to rehydrate (414 ml)

Rehydration of powdered potatoes is very fast, almost instant. It's more accurate to describe the potatoes as creamy potatoes rather than mashed. The texture is thick but not gluey. In addition to not puncturing vacuum bags, potato powder also takes up less space in a packed meal.

**Pot Cooking:** Since potato powder rehydrates almost instantly, it's best to soak the other ingredients for 5 minutes, and then bring them to a boil for a minute. Then stir in the potato powder and transfer the pot to an insulating cozy for 15 minutes. This requires that you pack the potato powder in a separate bag.

**Thermos Cooking:** Use 2 cups of boiled water (473 ml). Add to all ingredients in thermos, and wait 20 minutes or more.

# Rumbledethumps: Potatoes, Cabbage & Turnips

With a name like Rumbledethumps, this recipe from traditional Scottish fare has to be good.

The 2 main ingredients are potatoes and cabbage, but turnips and onions are often added. This version includes turnips, plus fresh chives instead of onions. Butter is also called for, but since the meal is dehydrated, we cook the cabbage in water with vegetable bouillon instead. For serving at home, shredded cheese is melted on top during the last 10 minutes in the oven.

**SERVINGS: 5**

**INGREDIENTS:**

2¼ lb. potatoes (approx.1 kg)

1 turnip (approx. 1 pound or 500 g)

½ white cabbage or green Savoy cabbage (approx. 1 pound or 500 g)

2 tsp. vegetable bouillon (10 g)

½ cup water (118 ml)

2 Tbsp. fresh chives

Salt and pepper to taste

**Additional ingredients (if not dehydrating the meal):** Use a liberal amount of butter, instead of water and bouillon, to sauté the cabbage. Add a few more pats of butter when mashing the potatoes and turnips. Add 1 cup shredded cheese on top during the last 10 minutes of baking.

## Cooking Rumbledethumps

Peel and chunk the potatoes and turnips. Cover with salted water (1 tsp. salt) and boil until soft, about 20 minutes.

While potatoes and turnips are cooking, sauté chopped cabbage in ½ cup water (118 ml) with 2 teaspoons of vegetable bouillon (10g) until the liquid evaporates, about 8 minutes.

When potatoes and turnips are soft, drain liquid. Return to pot, and hand mash with the cooked cabbage. Fold in chives after the mixture is mashed, and add salt and pepper to taste.

Preheat oven to 350°F (180°C).

Transfer Rumbledethumps to a baking dish and bake for 20 minutes.

If serving without dehydrating, top with shredded cheese after 20 minutes, and bake for an additional 10 minutes

## Dehydrating Rumbledethumps

This recipe makes 5½ cups of Rumbledethumps before drying. Spread 1 cup, plus a little more per tray. Dehydrate at 135°F (57°C) for 10–12 hours or until crispy. Break into smaller pieces when dry.

*A serving of reconstituted Rumbledethumps.*

**Servings:** 1

**Ingredients:** ¾ cup dried Rumbledethumps (50 g), 1 cup water (236 ml) to rehydrate.

**Pot Cooking:** Combine ¾ cup dried Rumbledethumps (50 g) with 1 cup water (236 ml) in pot, and soak for 5 minutes. Bring to a boil for 1 minute, and transfer pot to an insulating cozy for 15 minutes. Stir vigorously to return to mashed-potato consistency.

**Thermos Cooking:** Add 1¼–1½ cups boiled water (295–355 ml) to Rumbledethumps in thermos. Wait 20 minutes up to several hours. Shake thermos a couple of times.

If carrying a block of cheese, slice some on top before serving.

**Camping Scenario with Frying Pan:** Reconstitute and cook at camp as described above, then transfer Rumbledethumps to a skillet and fry in butter until browned. Top with cheddar cheese. Serve with grilled meat and vegetables.

To reconstitute the full yield of this recipe (5 servings), use 1 liter of water.

# Dehydrating Grated Potatoes

Steam small to medium-sized white potatoes with the skins on for 15 minutes. You want them to be fully cooked but not too soft. Cool cooked potatoes in a pot of cold water.

When potatoes are cool enough to handle, remove the skins.

Using a coarse grater, grate potatoes directly onto dehydrator trays covered with nonstick sheets. Move the grater across the dehydrator tray as you go to minimize having to separate the grated potatoes with your fingers. They will want to stick together, so a light touch with your fingers to finish spreading them around is best. If parts of your potatoes don't grate well, just set them aside, and eat them later. You will get a little of that when there is only a small amount of potato left between your fingers and the grater.

One Excalibur Dehydrator tray will hold approximately 1 pound of grated potatoes (454 g).

Dehydrate at 135°F (57°C) for 6–8 hours or until crispy. Flip the potatoes over after 4 hours to speed drying. They will hold together like a mat. Break into smaller pieces when dry.

**Yield:** 2 pounds of steamed and grated potatoes (907 g) yields 2½ cups dried (160 g).

## Grated Potatoes and Chili

**SERVINGS: 1 LARGE**

**INGREDIENTS:**

½ cup dried chili (45 g)

1 cup dried grated potatoes (64 g)

1¾ cups water to rehydrate (414 ml)

**Portion Option:** To make this a meatier and saucier meal, use more chili and less potatoes.

**Pot Cooking:** Combine dried chili and grated potatoes with water in pot, and soak for 5 minutes. Bring to a boil for 1 minute, then transfer pot to an insulating cozy for 15 minutes. Shake a little salt on meal as desired.

**Thermos Cooking:** Increase water by ¼ cup. Add 2 cups boiled water (473 ml) to the dried ingredients in thermos. Wait 20 minutes, up to several hours.

## Grated Potatoes with Sauerkraut & Ham

The tangy flavor and high sodium content of sauerkraut make it a dominant ingredient in this simple meal—you don't need any other spices or extra salt.

**SERVINGS: 1 LARGE**

**INGREDIENTS:**

¾ cup dried grated potatoes (48g)
⅓ cup dried sauerkraut (15 g)
⅓ cup dried ham (25 g)
1¾ cups water to rehydrate (414 ml)

**Pot Cooking:** Combine dried ingredients with water in pot, and soak for 5 minutes. Bring to a boil for 1 minute, then transfer pot to an insulating cozy for 15 minutes.

**Thermos Cooking:** Increase water by ¼ cup. Add 2 cups boiled water (473 ml) to the dried ingredients in thermos. Wait 20 minutes, up to several hours.

## Grated Potatoes with Vegetables & Meat

**Variations:** You can make many different potato-based meals just like this one. For example, in place of peas and carrots, you might include dried green beans or broccoli. A medley of dried onions, bell peppers, and mushrooms works too. In place of ground beef, you might include dried ground chicken or ham.

**SERVINGS: 1 LARGE**

**INGREDIENTS:**

¾ cup dried grated potatoes (48 g)
⅓ cup dried mixed vegetables (25 g)
⅓ cup dried ground beef (40 g)
Salt and pepper to taste
1¾ cups water to rehydrate (414 ml)

**Pot Cooking:** Combine dried ingredients with water in pot, and soak for 5 minutes. Bring to a boil for 1 minute, then transfer pot to an insulating cozy for 15 minutes. Shake a little salt and pepper on meal as desired.

**Thermos Cooking:** Increase water by ¼ cup. Add 2 cups boiled water (473 ml) to the dried ingredients in thermos. Wait 20 minutes, up to several hours.

# 7. Barley Recipes

## Beef & Barley with Fennel

Barley is a grain. The indigestible hull is removed during processing. If the bran layer and germ are kept intact, the barley is called "dehulled" or "pot" barley. More commonly, the bran layer and germ are steamed off, and the stripped grain is polished and packaged into what is called "pearl" barley. The barley you see floating in your Beef & Barley Soup, with little grooves down the centers, is pearl barley. This recipe uses pearl barley, which is what you usually find in stores.

*1 serving of rehydrated Beef & Barley.*

**SERVINGS: 4 REGULAR**

**INGREDIENTS:**

1 lb. lean ground beef (453 g)

1 cup pearl barley (200 g) + 2 tsp. bouillon (10 g)

1 large bulb fennel

1 red bell pepper

**Seasonings for Ground Beef:**

½ cup fine breadcrumbs or ground oats

1 Tbsp. bouillon

½ tsp. paprika

½ tsp. curry powder

¼ tsp. garlic powder

¼ tsp. onion powder

### Cooking Beef & Barley with Fennel

**Step 1: Season Ground Beef**

Combine breadcrumbs or ground oats and beef seasonings in a bowl, then mix it evenly into a pound of lean ground beef. Form the beef into a ball and set aside.

**Step 2: Cook Barley**

In a saucepot, combine 1 cup pearl barley (200 g) with 3 cups water (710 ml) and 1 tablespoon of bouillon. Bring to a boil, then reduce heat to a low simmer. Cook for 20 minutes, and then remove pot from heat.

You will use all of the cooked barley in the recipe.

**Step 3: Chop Fennel and Bell Pepper**

While the barley is cooking, chop the fennel into small pieces, and dice the bell pepper.

### Step 4: Cook Ground Beef and Vegetables

Pull apart the seasoned beef into small pieces. Place meat in a cold, nonstick pan. Begin heating pan on medium. This allows the meat to sweat out a tiny amount of grease so you don't need to oil the pan. Increase the heat to medium high and continue cooking, about 10 minutes with lots of stirring, until the meat is lightly browned and cooked through.

Add the fennel and bell pepper, and continue cooking at medium high for another 10 minutes, stirring frequently.

Place a lid over the pan, reduce heat to low, and simmer another 10 minutes.

### Step 5: Add Cooked Barley

Stir the cooked barley into the meat and vegetables. With the lid on the pan, continue cooking on low for, that's right…another 10 minutes, stirring once or twice. Lastly, remove lid, and allow food to cool.

## Dehydrating Beef & Barley with Fennel

This recipe yields 9–10 cups wet. Divide into 4 equal servings, and spread each on its own dehydrator tray covered with a nonstick sheet (2¼ to 2½ cups per tray).

Dehydrate at 145°F (63°C) for 10–12 hours or until no discernable moisture remains. Stir the contents of the tray occasionally to speed up drying.

*Dried Beef & Barley with Fennel from 1 dehydrator tray (1 serving).*

Wet volume and weight per serving: 2½ cups (420 g).

Dry volume and weight per serving: 1 cup (125 g).

**Servings:** 1

**Pot Cooking:** Combine 1 cup dried Beef & Barley (125 g) with 1¼ cups water (236 ml) in pot. Let soak 5 minutes, then bring to a boil for 1 minute. Transfer pot to an insulating cozy for 15 minutes.

**Thermos Cooking:** Use ¼ cup more water. Place 1 cup dried Beef & Barley (125 g) in thermos food jar and add 1½ cups boiled water (355 ml). Wait 20 minutes, up to several hours.

## Beef & Barley Soup

**Servings:** 1

**Pot Cooking:** Combine ½ cup dried Beef & Barley (63 g) and 1 tablespoon (10 g) of powdered bouillon with 2 cups of water (473 ml) in pot. Let soak 5 minutes, then bring to a boil for 1 minute. Transfer pot to an insulating cozy for 15 minutes.

**Thermos Cooking:** Combine ½ cup (63 g) of dried Beef & Barley and 1 tablespoon (10 g) of powdered bouillon with 2 cups of boiled water (473 ml) in thermos food jar. Wait 20 minutes, up to several hours.

With either method, add a pinch of salt when serving if needed.

# Barley Risotto with Peas & Mushrooms

**SERVINGS: 2 LARGE**

**INGREDIENTS:**

1 cup pearl barley (200 g)
1½ cups frozen peas (200 g)
6 oz. mushrooms (170 g)
1 green onion
1 clove garlic
1 handful fresh parsley
½ Tbsp. cooking oil
4 cups vegetable broth (946 ml)
¼ cup white wine
1 Tbsp. Worcestershire sauce
½ Tbsp. balsamic vinegar
¼ tsp. garlic powder
¼ tsp. salt (or to taste)

## Cooking Barley Risotto with Peas & Mushrooms

**Step 1: Prepare the Vegetables**

Slice mushrooms, trim stems from parsley, chop green onion, and press or mince garlic.

**Step 2: Cook the Mushrooms**

Place mushrooms and parsley in a pan. Add 1 tablespoon of Worcestershire sauce, ½ tablespoon of balsamic vinegar, and ¼ teaspoon of garlic powder (or use fresh garlic). Cook for 3 minutes, and remove from heat.

**Step 3: Cook the Peas**

Bring 4 cups of vegetable broth (910 ml) to a boil. (A tablespoon of powdered vegetable bouillon (10 g) was used to make the broth. Chicken broth may be substituted.) Add peas, and cook for 3 minutes. Strain peas over another large bowl, retaining the broth to cook the barley in. Combine peas with the cooked mushrooms, and add salt and pepper to taste.

**Step 4: Cook the Barley Risotto-Style**

In a large pan coated with ½ tablespoon of cooking oil, cook green onion and garlic for 3 minutes over medium-high heat.

Add barley, stirring continuously for 5 minutes.

Add white wine, and stir barley until wine is absorbed. If you don't want to use wine, use vegetable broth instead. Continue adding vegetable broth, ½ cup at a time, allowing it to absorb into the barley each time. Once you've added all of the broth, the barley should have cooked to an al dente texture.

Add peas and mushrooms to cooked barley, and simmer on low for 5 more minutes.

## Dehydrating Barley Risotto with Peas & Mushrooms

Divide meal into 2 equal portions, and spread on 2 trays covered with nonstick sheets.

Dehydrate at 135°F (57°C) for 8–10 hours or until no moisture remains.

**Yield:** This recipe yields slightly more than 2 cups of dried barley risotto (290 g). Divide into 2 equal portions, approximately 1 cup each (145 g). This is a very filling serving size.

*Dehydrated Barley Risotto with Peas & Mushrooms.*

**Servings:** 1

**Pot Cooking:** Combine 1 cup dried Barley Risotto with Peas & Mushrooms (145 g) with 1¼ cups water (236 ml) in pot. Let soak 5 minutes, then bring to a boil for 1 minute. Transfer pot to an insulating cozy for 15 to 20 minutes. Peas like a little more time to rehydrate.

**Thermos Cooking:** Use ¼ cup more water. Place 1 cup dried Barley Risotto with Peas & Mushrooms (145 g) in thermos food jar, and add 1½ cups boiled water (355 ml). Wait 20 minutes, up to several hours.

Sprinkle parmesan cheese over the meal when serving if desired.

Dried Barley Risotto with Peas & Mushrooms can also be rehydrated as a soup. *See next page.*

## Barley with Peas & Mushrooms Soup

**Servings:** 1

**Pot Cooking:** Combine ½ cup dried Barley Risotto (72 g) and 1 tablespoon of powdered bouillon (10 g), with 2 cups of water (473 ml) in pot. Let soak 5 minutes, then bring to a boil for 1 minute. Transfer pot to an insulating cozy for 15 to 20 minutes.

**Thermos Cooking:** Combine ½ cup dried Barley Risotto (72 g) and 1 tablespoon of powdered bouillon (10 g), with 2 cups of boiled water (473 ml) in thermos. Wait 30 minutes, up to several hours.

With either method, add a pinch of salt when serving if needed.

# 8. Macaroni & Tomato Sauce

## Dehydrating Macaroni

In the first *Recipes for Adventure,* the macaroni recipes call for using macaroni straight from a box of mac and cheese. When macaroni meals are cooked in a pot, and a boil is maintained for 2 minutes, followed by insulating the meal in a pot cozy for 10 to 15 minutes, the macaroni turns out fine. Macaroni from boxed mac and cheese is fairly thin, so it cooks quickly.

For other types of trail meal preparation, such as freezer-bag cooking or cold soaking, you should precook and dehydrate the macaroni. You can use standard-sized macaroni; it is not necessary to use macaroni from a box of mac and cheese.

Precooked-and-dried macaroni rehydrates well when boiled water is added to it in a freezer bag, as long as you insulate the meal in a pouch cozy for 20 minutes. When dried macaroni is cooked in a pot, you no longer have to maintain a boil for 2 minutes—1 minute will do.

For making cold pasta salads, precooked-and-dried macaroni rehydrates well with cold water. However, a soak time of more than 1 hour is required. A thermos food jar works great for this. Add the dried ingredients and cold water in the morning; enjoy the meal for lunch.

### Precooking and Dehydrating Macaroni

For each cup of macaroni (100 g) to be cooked, add 1 teaspoon of salt to a quart or liter of water and bring it to a rapid boil. Add the macaroni, and reduce heat to maintain a gentle boil.

Slightly undercook the macaroni. If the instructions on the box say to boil the macaroni for 8 minutes, strain off the water at 7 minutes.

*Cooked macaroni on mesh sheet of dehydrator tray.*

Immediately rinse the macaroni in cold water to stop the cooking. Rinsing also ensures that the macaroni will not stick together on the dehydrator tray.

Spread the cooked macaroni out on dehydrator trays in 1 layer. There is no need to use a nonstick sheet, as that would only slow down dehydration.

Dehydrate at 135°F (57°C) for 4–6 hours or until macaroni is hard.

½ cup dried macaroni (47 g) on left. On right, rehydrated with ¼ cup boiled water (59 ml) in a thermos for 10 minutes. Surprisingly little water is required to bring the macaroni back to its original al dente texture.

## Tips for Rehydrating Precooked-and-Dried Macaroni Meals

**Pot Cooking:** Add macaroni with other dried ingredients to pot with required water for recipe. Soak 5 minutes, then bring to a boil for 1 minute. Transfer pot to insulating cozy for 15 minutes. For easier cleanup, stir in milk and cheese powders after you take the pot off the stove.

**Thermos Cooking:** Add boiled water to ingredients in thermos. Wait 20 minutes, up to several hours. If preparing the meal in the morning to eat later for lunch, add an extra ¼ cup water since the dried ingredients will have more time to absorb it.

(Left) Chili mac soaked in thermos for 3 hours; (right) chili mac also soaked for 3 hours, but the mac was added 30 minutes before serving. The mac on the right was perfect al dente; on the left, it was softer.

When soaked in boiled water for several hours, macaroni will get soft. It still tastes good, and it is convenient to add all the dried ingredients at the same time. If you want perfect al dente texture, wait until 30 minutes before serving to add the macaroni to the thermos.

**Cold Soak:** Add cold water to the dried ingredients, and wait at least an hour, but 2 to 3 hours is better. If you prepare the meal in the morning to eat later for lunch, a thermos food jar will keep it cold.

*See **Beefy Macaroni & Tomato Sauce** on page 87, and **Tuna & Macaroni San Marzano**, on page 88.*

# Homemade Tomato-Sauce Powder

To make the most flavorful tomato-sauce powder, cook a batch of well-seasoned tomato sauce first. Dried tomatoes can also be ground into powder, but they won't include the built-in taste that you can simmer into a sauce. If you're not inclined to make your own sauce, you can make tomato-sauce powder from store-bought tomato sauce.

Roma and San Marzano tomatoes are meaty and make good sauce. Since it is sometimes hard to find ripe tomatoes at the store, tomato sauce can also be made from canned diced tomatoes.

**Main Ingredient:** 6 14.5-ounce cans of diced tomatoes (2.4 kg) or 5½ pounds fresh tomatoes (2.5 kg).

**SEASONING INGREDIENTS:**

- 1 Tbsp. garlic powder
- 2 tsp. salt
- 2 tsp. sugar
- 1 tsp. onion powder
- ½ tsp. pepper
- 1 tsp. red pepper flakes
- 1½ Tbsp. dried basil
- 2 tsp. dried oregano
- 2 tsp. dried parsley
- 4 bay leaves
- 2 Tbsp. red wine vinegar

## Cooking Tomato Sauce

**Blend the Tomatoes**
Run diced tomatoes through a blender to a smoothielike consistency. It will take 2 fills.

**Season the Sauce**
Transfer sauce to a stockpot, and add all seasonings. Red pepper flakes give this sauce a bit of heat. Use less if you desire a mellower sauce.

**Cook the Sauce**
Bring sauce to a light boil over medium-high heat, then reduce heat to low. Simmer uncovered for 1 hour. Sauce will thicken as liquid evaporates. Once the sauce is thick, allow it to cool.

## Dehydrating Sauce into Tomato-Sauce Leather

This recipe yields 5 to 6 cups of thick sauce, which can be dried on 5 Excalibur Dehydrator trays. Remove bay leaves. Spread between 1 and 1¼ cups of tomato sauce thinly on each dehydrator tray covered with a nonstick sheet. Caution: spreading too much sauce on a tray will make a thick leather that will take longer to dry and won't reduce to tomato-sauce powder as well.

Dehydrate at 135°F (57°C) for 10–12 hours or longer.

After 8 hours, the tomato-sauce leather should be dry enough to remove the nonstick sheets. Flip the nonstick sheets over onto the mesh sheets, and peel the nonstick sheets away from the leather. Finish drying on the mesh sheets.

The drying time to make leather that will be ground into tomato-sauce powder is a couple hours longer than the time required to dry tomato-sauce leather that will be used as is. When completely dry, you should be able to easily snap or tear it into smaller pieces.

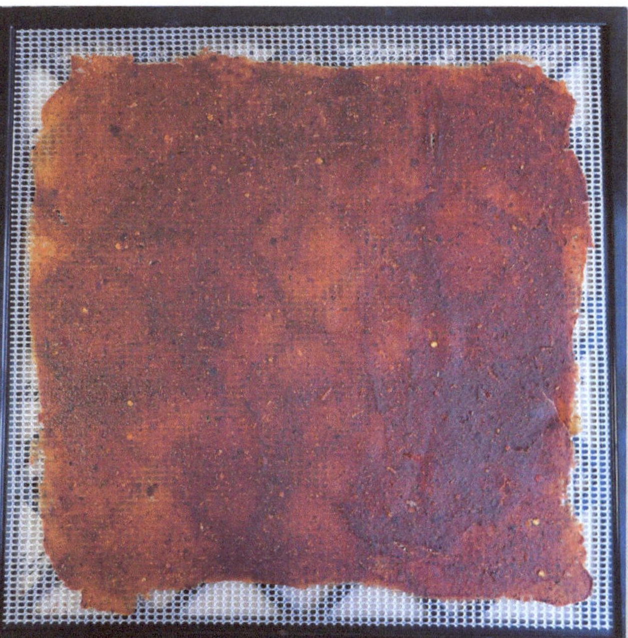

*(Left) Tomato sauce spread thinly on dehydrator tray covered with nonstick sheet; (right) dried sauce after being flipped over with nonstick sheet removed.*

## Grinding Tomato-Sauce Leather into Tomato-Sauce Powder

Tear leather into smaller pieces and reduce to tomato-sauce powder in a blender. Work with small quantities so as not to overheat your blender.

⅓ cup of tomato-sauce leather (25 g) reduced to 2½ Tbsp. of tomato-sauce powder (25 g).

Backpacking recipes in the first *Recipes for Adventure* call for either ¼ or ⅓ cup tomato-sauce leather, depending on the serving size. The chart below shows the equivalent amount of tomato-sauce powder to use.

**Tomato-Sauce Leather to Tomato-Sauce Powder Conversions**

- ¼ cup leather (20 g) = 2 Tbsp. powder (20 g)
- ⅓ cup leather (25 g) = 2½ Tbsp. powder (25 g)

The total yield of this tomato-sauce powder recipe, which starts with 6 14.5-ounce cans of diced tomatoes, is approximately 24 tablespoons of tomato-sauce powder, enough for 10–12 backpacking meals that call for sauce.

## Reconstituting Tomato-Sauce Powder for Home Use

2½ tablespoons of tomato-sauce powder rehydrated back into thick sauce with ½ cup boiled water.

Combine ¼ cup tomato-sauce powder (40 g) with 1¼ cups of water (295 ml). Bring to a light boil, and then remove pot from heat. Wait 15 minutes or longer. Sauce thickens with time. Add more water a tablespoon at a time for a thinner sauce. Stir in a spoonful of extra-virgin olive oil if desired. This amount will be enough for 2–3 servings of pasta, depending on how saucy you like your pasta.

# Beefy Macaroni & Tomato Sauce

*Rehydrated Beefy Macaroni & Vegetables in Tomato Sauce.*

**1 REGULAR SERVING:**

½ cup dried macaroni (50 g)
¼ cup dried ground beef (30 g)
¼ cup dried vegetables (20 g)
2 Tbsp. tomato-sauce powder (24 g)
1½ cups water to rehydrate (355 ml)

**1 LARGE SERVING:**

¾ cup dried macaroni (70 g)
⅓ cup dried ground beef (40 g)
⅓ cup dried vegetables (25 g)
3 Tbsp. tomato-sauce powder (36 g)
2¼ cups water to rehydrate (532 ml)

For vegetables, try a mix of dried bell peppers and dried olives. Dried mushrooms are good too.

**Optional:** Include a packet of parmesan cheese for a topping.

**Pot Cooking:** Combine all ingredients with water in pot, and soak for 5 minutes. Bring to a boil for 1 minute. Transfer pot to an insulating cozy for 15 minutes.

**Thermos Cooking:** Use ¼–½ cup more water if making the meal in the morning to eat for lunch. Add boiled water to ingredients in thermos. Wait at least 20 minutes, up to several hours. For perfect al dente macaroni, don't add the macaroni to the thermos until 30 minutes before serving. If macaroni sits for several hours in a thermos with hot water, it tends to get soft. It still tastes good, either way.

# 9. Cold-Soak Salads

## Tuna & Macaroni San Marzano

This no-cook backpacking recipe is perfect for lunch on a hot summer day. All the ingredients, except the tuna, are dehydrated. It's important to use precooked-and-dried macaroni; otherwise the macaroni will not be palatable if rehydrated in cold water.

*(Left) Dried ingredients for Tuna & Macaroni San Marzano; (right) rehydrated with cold water for 2½ hours in a thermos food jar.*

**SERVINGS: 1**

**INGREDIENTS:**

- ½ cup precooked-and-dried macaroni (50 g)
- ¼ cup dried San Marzano tomato pieces (10 g)
- ¼ cup dried green beans (5 g)
- 1 Tbsp. dried olives (5 g)
- 2.6-oz. packet of tuna (74 g)
- ¾ cup water to rehydrate (177 ml)

**Cold Preparation:** Add dried ingredients and cold water to thermos food jar or other container with a tight-fitting lid. Wait at least 2 hours; 2.5 hours is ideal for this recipe. Stir in tuna; enjoy! Tip: Prepare this meal in the morning before you break camp.

**Hot Preparation:** Add all ingredients to pot with water. Bring to a boil for 1 minute. Transfer pot to insulating cozy for 15 minutes.

*See **Dehydrating Olives** next page, **Dehydrating Macaroni** on page 82, and **Dehydrating San Marzano Tomatoes** on page 90.*

# Dehydrating Olives

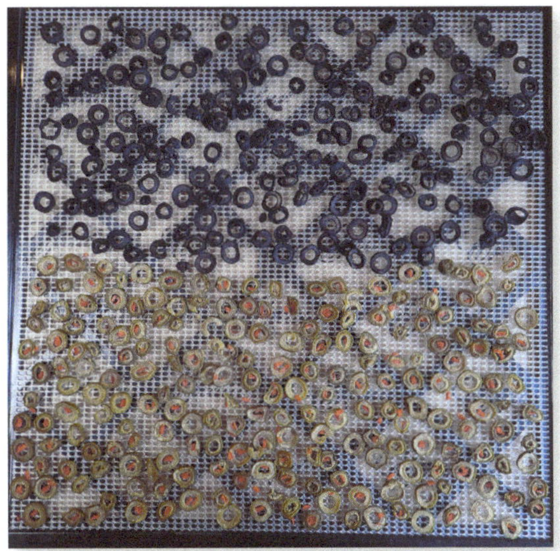

Perk up your trail snacks and meals with dehydrated olives. Use either black or green olives. Save time: buy them with the pits already removed.

Olives are usually preserved in a brine solution. That makes them very salty. Before dehydrating olives, rinse them in cold water to reduce some of the salt.

Slice olives crosswise 3 or 4 times. Arrange in a single layer on mesh dehydrator sheet.

Dehydrate at 135°F (57°C) for 8–10 hours or until they are dry enough to snap in half. Start drying olives at a higher temperature for the first 2 hours to speed up drying.

When fully dried, olives easily break in half rather than bend. You can fit 12 ounces of sliced olives (350 g) on 1 Excalibur Dehydrator tray.

## Dehydrating Olive Paste for Tortillas

Another way to dehydrate olives is to run them through a blender first. Dried olive powder can be reconstituted quickly in cold water to use as a spread on tortillas.

Add ½ cup water (118 ml) to 7 ounces of rinsed olives (200 g) in a blender. Add a pinch of garlic powder if desired. Blend until smooth. This will make approximately 1 cup of blended olives.

Spread thinly on dehydrator tray covered with nonstick sheet.

Dehydrate at 135°F (57°C) for 8–10 hours or until dry. Olive bark can be easily crumbled by hand into olive powder.

**Yield:** 1 cup of blended olives yields approximately ½ cup of olive powder (40 g).

Reconstitute olive powder with an equal quantity of cold water. The photo shows 2 tablespoons of olive powder on the left and reconstituted with 2 tablespoons of cold water on right. Spread 2 tablespoons of reconstituted olive powder on 1 8-inch tortilla. You don't need any more, as it is strong in flavor and saltiness. Add your favorite meats or cheeses and fold the tortilla in half.

# Dehydrating San Marzano Tomatoes

A great way to dehydrate tomatoes is to dry them in halves. San Marzano tomatoes, with their oblong shape and meaty texture, are perfect tomatoes for drying. Big Boy and Better Boy tomatoes are too fat to dry in halves; they are better suited to dicing or slicing.

The benefit of drying tomatoes with the half cut is that all of the flavors in the juice remain inside the tomatoes as they dry. It takes several hours longer to dry tomatoes this way, but the taste will amaze you. They make great snacks; you could call it tomato jerky. The dried halves can also be cut into smaller pieces to use in meals.

## Dehydrating Tomatoes Using the Half-Cut Method

*San Marzano tomatoes (left to right): 1. Cut in half. 2. White part removed. 3. Seasoned.*

Cut tomatoes in half lengthwise.

Using a sharp knife, cut out white pithy sections between both ends of the tomatoes, being careful not to cut all the way through the tomatoes. If you leave the pithy section in there, it tends to dry hard.

After you cut out the white part, sprinkle seasonings onto each tomato half, and then gently push the seasonings down into the juicy middle sections of the tomatoes with a knife or spoon.

## Seasoning Mix for Tomatoes

**INGREDIENTS FOR 24 TOMATOES:**

- 1 tsp. salt
- 1 tsp. basil
- 1 tsp. oregano
- ½ tsp. garlic powder
- ¼ tsp. pepper
- 2 Tbsp. red wine vinegar (add last)

Add any seasonings that you like. The mix at left will give the tomatoes an Italian flair, and your kitchen will smell like a pizzeria while the tomatoes are drying.

Add the dry seasonings to a bowl, and rub them between your fingers to mix the flavors well. Sprinkle as desired onto tomatoes, and push the seasoning into the juices with a knife or spoon. Add 1 or 2 drops of red wine vinegar to each tomato after you add the dry seasonings.

## Dehydrating San Marzano Tomatoes

Dehydrate at 135°F (57°C) for 15–18 hours or more.

Times will vary depending on the thickness of the tomatoes and other factors like humidity in the surrounding environment. A dehydrator with a fan is a must, or the tomatoes won't dry properly.

If noticeable moisture remains in the tomato halves after 16 hours, cut them into smaller pieces, and continue drying.

Because the tomato halves are thicker than diced or sliced tomatoes, you may only be able to use every other tray in your dehydrator.

*(Left) 12 tomatoes, cut side up, on dehydrator tray; (right) dried tomatoes after 15 hours.*

## Dried San Marzano Tomatoes Make Great Trail Snacks

Pack dried tomato halves whole, or cut them into smaller pieces with scissors. Dried San Marzano tomatoes and dried olives make a tasty trail mix.

# Couscous Salad with Cucumber-Salsa Dressing

*Rehydrated Couscous Salad with Cucumber-Salsa Dressing.*

Couscous Salad makes a refreshing lunch when rehydrated with cold water ahead of time. This recipe includes a dehydrated cucumber-salsa dressing. A thermos food jar will keep the meal cold while it rehydrates, but any container with a tight lid will do. Vegetables take longer to rehydrate in cold water than in boiled water, so allow at least 2 hours of soak time.

Use a medley of dried vegetables and legumes in the salad for a variety of colors and textures.

## Drying Beans and Vegetables

Steam peas, corn, and carrots for 6 minutes before drying.

Dehydrate at 125°F (52°C).

Tomatoes dry faster at 135°F (57°C).

**Estimated Drying Times:**

6–8 hr. beans, chickpeas, peas

10–12 hr. corn, carrots

12–14 hr. cucumbers, tomatoes, bell peppers

*(Left to right) chickpeas, kidney beans, corn, peas, cucumbers, tomatoes, red bell peppers, and carrots.*

## Cucumber-Salsa Dressing

**SERVINGS: 3–4**

**INGREDIENTS:**

1 lb. cucumbers, peeled and diced (454 g)
½ cup salsa
Juice from ½ lemon
Handful of fresh herbs (cilantro, basil, chives)

## Dehydrating Cucumber-Salsa Dressing

Run all ingredients through bender until smooth. Spread thinly on dehydrator trays covered with nonstick sheets. This recipe took up 1 Excalibur Dehydrator tray.

Dehydrate at 135°F (57°C) for 10–12 hours. Expect leather to turn light brown, since cucumbers are prone to oxidation. Leather will easily tear into pieces.

## Couscous Salad with Cucumber-Salsa Dressing

**SERVINGS: 1**

**INGREDIENTS:**

½ cup couscous (80 g)

½ cup dried mixed vegetables and beans (50 g)

¼ cup cucumber-salsa leather (10g)

2 cups water to rehydrate (473 ml)

Combine all ingredients with cold water. Wait at least 2 hours to serve, but 3 hours is better. Add a little olive oil when serving.

# Quinoa & Bean Cilantro Salad

Quinoa, pronounced "keen-wa," possesses 9 essential amino acids, making it a complete protein. It has a slightly nutty taste and can be used in place of rice in backpacking recipes.

## Cooking Quinoa

The recipe calls for 3 cups of cooked red quinoa. One cup of quinoa seeds will produce the 3 cups you need. Begin by rinsing the seeds several times to remove any remaining saponins, which taste bitter.

Add 2 cups of water (473 ml), seasoned with ¼ teaspoon of salt and a chip of bouillon, to 1 cup of quinoa seeds (180 g).

Bring to a boil, then reduce heat to low, and cover pot. Quinoa should be done in 30 minutes, and all water will have been absorbed. Let the quinoa cool while you work on the other ingredients.

If you use canned beans, all you have to cook is the quinoa. The other ingredients—tomatoes, bell peppers, onions, and garlic—go in raw. Cilantro, cumin, and fresh lime juice give this salad a bright salsa aroma and taste.

Fresh-cut cilantro leaves are essential in this recipe. Use more than called for if you love it!

## Preparing Quinoa & Bean Cilantro Salad

**SERVINGS: 8, 1 CUP EACH**

**INGREDIENTS:**

3 cups cooked quinoa (from 1 cup quinoa seeds)
1 can red or black beans, rinsed (310 g)
1 small can corn, rinsed (170 g)
4 tomatoes, seeded and diced
1 orange bell pepper, diced
1 small green onion, including green stalk, diced*
1 small red onion, diced
1–2 cloves garlic, minced
½ cup cilantro leaves, cut smaller
1 lime, juice only
1 Tbsp. red wine vinegar
1½ tsp. ground cumin
¾ tsp. salt
½ tsp. paprika or cayenne pepper

**Optional:** Add something hot, like red or green chilies or jalapeno peppers. Use sparingly. If you don't have a green onion on hand, use more red onion. Diced yellow bell pepper can be substituted as a yellow ingredient for corn.

Cut the white cores out of the center of the tomatoes, then quarter them. To remove the tomato seeds, scrape out the seeds and push them through a strainer. Add the liberated tomato juices to the corn and beans.

Dice tomatoes, bell pepper, onions, and garlic. Cut cilantro leaves into smaller pieces.

Add to bowl with quinoa, beans, corn, and seasonings.

If you're not going to dehydrate the salad, chill it in the refrigerator until ready to serve.

**Yield:** 8½ cups of Quinoa & Bean Cilantro Salad, a perfect quantity to take to your next potluck. If you dehydrate the whole batch, the dried volume will be approximately 4½ cups.

## Dehydrating Quinoa & Bean Cilantro Salad

Dehydrate at 135°F (57°C) for 10–12 hours using nonstick sheets. If using an Excalibur Dehydrator, 2 cups of wet salad fit nicely on 1 tray.

*Quinoa & Bean Cilantro Salad before and after drying.*

## Rehydrating Quinoa & Bean Cilantro Salad

Rehydrate with cold water, and wait 3 or more hours. Cold-water rehydration takes longer than hot-water rehydration. The wait time is perfect for filling a thermos food jar, or other container with a tight-fitting lid, in the morning to enjoy the salad for lunch.

**Large Serving:** Combine a little more than 1 cup dried salad (95 g) with 1 cup cold water (237 ml). This equates to 2 cups of the salad that was dried on 1 tray.

**What to expect:** With its fragrant ingredients, this salad wakes up the taste buds nicely. It does not absorb as much water as was lost during dehydration. There may be a little free juice remaining after rehydration, but it will be flavorful.

# Shrimp-Cocktail Tortillas

You can dehydrate jarred cocktail sauce, or make your own with the following recipe.

## Homemade Shrimp-Cocktail Sauce

**MAKES 2 CUPS OF COCKTAIL SAUCE FOR 2.2 POUNDS OF SHRIMP (1 KG).**

**INGREDIENTS:**

1 15-oz. can whole or diced tomatoes (400 g)
3 Tbsp. tomato paste
1 lemon (juice and zest)
6 Tbsp. grated horseradish root*
2 tsp. Worcestershire sauce
¾ tsp. Tabasco sauce
¾ tsp. salt
2 oz. cooked shrimp pieces (50 g), to thicken sauce

*Horseradish: Grate fresh from a root, or use prepared horseradish from a jar. Start with less, taste as you go, and add more horseradish to suit your heat preference.

Place all ingredients in a blender, and blend just until smooth. Set aside.

## Preparing the Shrimp

Use 1 kilogram (2.2 pounds) of frozen precooked shrimp—the kind you buy for shrimp cocktail, with the tails still on.

Thaw shrimp, remove tails, and cut it into small pieces. Split each shrimp in half lengthwise along the vein channel, and then make 4 or 5 cuts crosswise.

Combine 2 cups of cocktail sauce with 2.2 pounds of cut shrimp (1 kg).

*Dehydrating Shrimp Cocktail, before and after.*

## Dehydrating Shrimp Cocktail

Place shrimp mixed with cocktail sauce on dehydrator trays covered with nonstick sheets.

Dehydrate at 145°F (63°C) for 6–8 hours or until crispy.

After 4 hours of drying, pull apart the shrimp cocktail, rearrange it loosely on the tray, and continue drying.

**Yield:** The dry weight of 2.2 pounds of shrimp (1 kg) mixed with 2 cups of cocktail sauce will be approximately 228 grams, about 3 cups.

**Packing:** ¾ cup dried shrimp cocktail (57 g) will fill 2 tortillas.

## Rehydrating Shrimp Cocktail (3–4 hour soak)

A 2-tortilla serving makes a hearty lunch for 1 person. For 2 tortillas, combine ¾ cup dried shrimp cocktail (57 g) with ¾ cup cold water (177 ml) in thermos food jar or other container with a tight-fitting lid.

After 3 or 4 hours, stir the shrimp cocktail, and fold it into 2 tortillas. The shrimp cocktail is refreshingly spicy with a chewy texture.

Dried shrimp cocktail also goes well in hot or cold meals when combined with dried rice and green bell peppers.

# Sushi Rice Bowl Salad

This no-cook backpacking meal includes dehydrated sushi rice, cucumbers, and surimi. It's like a California sushi roll in a bowl, without the avocado. You can add fresh avocado on the trail, but don't bother dehydrating avocado, because it turns brown and doesn't rehydrate well.

*(Above) Sushi rice salad rehydrated with cold water in thermos food jar, (below) dried cucumber, surimi, and sushi rice.*

**SERVINGS: 1**

**INGREDIENTS:**

¾ cup dried sushi rice (80 g)
¼ cup dried surimi (20 g)
¼ cup dried cucumber (10 g)
1 cup cold water to rehydrate (253 ml)

For a larger serving, use 100 grams sushi rice, 25 grams surimi, 12 grams cucumber, and 1¼ cups cold water. Use a little more water for longer soak times.

Combine ingredients with cold water in thermos. For best results, wait at least 1½ hours. If waiting longer, rehydrate with a little extra water.

## Cooking Sushi Rice

Sushi rice is a short-grain rice which is cooked with less water than is used to cook long-grain rice. If available, choose Japanese sushi rice. Rice vinegar is added to the rice after it is cooked.

The ingredients needed to make sushi rice, besides the short-grain rice, are rice vinegar, sugar, and salt. Check the ingredients list of the rice vinegar you buy; it may already include sugar or salt. The rice vinegar used for this recipe included sugar, but no salt.

If the rice vinegar contains no salt or sugar, add those items to the rice vinegar in a pot and heat on low temperature until the salt and sugar dissolve. You can do this while the rice is cooking. Overheating the rice vinegar will cause a loss of flavor. That is why you don't add it to the rice until after the rice is cooked.

For 1¼ cups (250 g) of sushi rice, use 5 tablespoons of rice vinegar, 2½ teaspoons sugar, and 1 teaspoon salt. Leave out salt or sugar if already present in the rice vinegar.

Rinse rice several times with cool water. The water will turn chalky at first due to the high starch content of the rice. After rinsing, soak rice in cooking water for 30 minutes.

Cook 1¼ cup sushi rice (250 g) with 1½ cup water (350 ml). Bring to a boil, then reduce heat to a low simmer for 10 minutes with the lid on the pot.

After 10 minutes, turn off the stove, and let the rice sit for 15 minutes, keeping the lid on the pot.

**Important:** Don't let any steam escape by lifting the lid off the pot. Your patience will be rewarded with perfect sushi rice.

When you finally lift the lid after the 15-minute wait, drizzle the rice vinegar/salt/sugar solution over the rice and gently mix it in with a folding motion using a wooden spoon if you have one.

**Next page: Dehydrating Sushi Rice.**

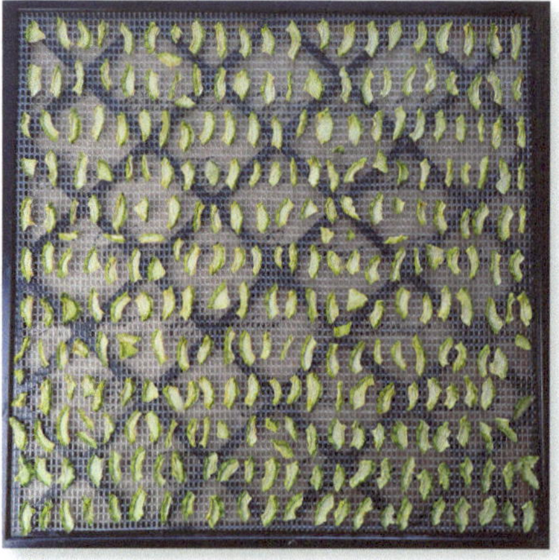

## Dehydrating Sushi Rice

After you mix in the rice vinegar, and the rice has cooled a bit, place it on dehydrator trays covered with nonstick sheets. Since the rice sticks together, place 1 teaspoonful of rice at a time on the trays, leaving space between the little piles. Then, spread the little piles out a little more.

Dehydrate at 145°F (63°C) for 4-6 hours.

When rice is almost dry, pull apart some of the rice that is sticking together and redistribute on the trays. Rice will be hard when dry.

**Yield:** 1¼ cup sushi rice (250 g) yields 2¼ cup dried rice (240 g) after cooking and dehydrating.

## Dehydrating Surimi

*See **Dehydrating Surimi**, page 68.*

## Dehydrating Cucumbers

Peel cucumber, cut in half longwise, and scrape out seeds with a spoon. The central part of cucumbers surrounding the seeds tends to oxidize (turn brown) while drying, so you'll have better-looking dried cucumbers if you remove that part.

Slice the cucumber halves one more time so you have four quarters, and then slice crosswise ⅛–¼ inch thick (½ cm). To reduce browning even more after cutting, cucumbers may be dipped in a solution of 1 cup water and ¼ cup lemon juice.

Dehydrate at 135°F (57°C) for 7–8 hours. Dried cucumber will be pliable.

**Yield:** 1¼ large cucumbers (1 lb. after processing) will yield ¾ cup (23 g) when dry.

*(Top two): Dehydrating sushi rice, before and after.*

*(Bottom two): Dehydrating cucumbers, before and after. Quantity on one Excalibur dehydrator tray was 1¼ large cucumbers.*

# Peach Salsa Rice Salad

This salsa makes a delicious offering at any party—next to a bowl of tortilla chips—or you can dehydrate it for the trail. Rehydrate it by itself, or combine it with rice for a zesty rice salad.

**SERVINGS (WET): 11 CUPS.**

**INGREDIENTS:**

2 lb. diced tomatoes (900 g)
1¾ lb. diced peaches (800 g)
10 oz. diced bell peppers (290 g)
5 oz. diced onion (150 g)
2 diced cayenne peppers (20 g)
1 bunch cilantro, chopped (15 g)
1 lime, juiced
2 tsp. salt
½ tsp. pepper

**Optional:** 1–2 Tbsp. apricot or peach jam (20–40 g)

*Cayenne pepper.*

## Salsa Preparation

Dice all vegetables and mix together with salt and pepper. Remove seeds from peppers before dicing.

Cayenne peppers are moderately-hot chili peppers, usually red in color with a skinny shape. They are suitable for dishes served to mixed-company where you don't want to risk causing discomfort to sensitive tongues. If you like your salsa hot-hot, you may substitute a hotter pepper.

Cut a lime in half. Press and rotate the halves over a handheld juicer. Place the juiced contents in a bowl.

Peel and dice peaches. Place the diced peaches in the bowl with the lime juice as you work. Stir to coat peaches. Tip: Select ripe peaches with firm flesh. Overripe peaches will be harder to dice.

Depending on how sweet the peaches are, add one or two tablespoons of peach or apricot jam to the peaches.

Combine diced vegetables and peaches, and add chopped cilantro.

Let salsa sit for a few minutes, stirring to mix the flavors.

*Dehydrating peach salsa: before and after.*

## Dehydrating Peach Salsa

Spread salsa in a single layer on dehydrator trays covered with nonstick sheets. This recipe provides a little more than 2 cups of salsa on each of 5 trays. Include juices equally on trays.

Dehydrate at 135°F (57°C) for 15 to 18 hours. You can speed up drying by starting at 145°F (63°C) for 3 hours.

**Active Dehydrating Tips:** After 12 hours, peel salsa off nonstick sheets and redistribute. For the final hour, transfer almost dried salsa from 5 trays down to 2 trays. This will increase air flow.

**Dried Yield:** 11 cups (wet) yields 3 cups dry (229 g).

## Cooking and Dehydrating Short-grain Rice

Dehydrated short-grain rice rehydrates great in cold water. Use the same rice as was used to make the sushi rice salad. Cook and dehydrate the same way, but cook the rice in salted water and omit the rice vinegar and sugar.

Rinse rice several times with cool water. The water will turn chalky at first due to the high starch content of the rice. After rinsing, soak rice in cooking water for 30 minutes.

**Double Portion:**

For 2½ cups of short-grain rice (500 g), use 2 teaspoons of salt and 3 cups of water (710 ml).

Bring to a boil, then reduce heat to a low simmer for 10 minutes with the lid on the pot.

After 10 minutes, turn off the stove, and let the rice sit for 15 minutes, keeping the lid on the pot.

**Yield:** 2½ cups short-grain rice (500 g) will yield 4½ cups dried rice (470 g) after cooking and dehydrating.

Peach Salsa Rice Salad rehydrated in thermos food jar.

### Rehydrating Peach Salsa Rice Salad

**Regular Serving:** ¾ cup dried short-grain rice (80 g), and ½ cup dried peach salsa (40 g). Rehydrate with 1 cup cold water (236 ml).

**Large Serving:** 1 cup dried short-grain rice (100 g), and ⅔ cup dried peach salsa (50 g). Rehydrate with 1¼ cup cold water (300 ml).

After adding water, wait at least 1 hour, but 1½–2 hours is best. For longer soak times, rehydrate with a little more water. A thermos food jar is the best way to rehydrate this no-cook backpacking meal. You want this zesty meal to be cold and refreshing on a hot summer's day.

To rehydrate peach salsa by itself without rice, cover with cold water in a container and hike on. After 1 or 2 hours, enjoy as a snack with tortilla chips, or add it to a packet of tuna or chicken.

## Peach Salsa Corn Salad

For an exciting variation, use dehydrated corn in place of dehydrated rice.

Peach Salsa Corn Salad rehydrated in thermos food jar.

### Rehydrating Peach Salsa Corn Salad

**Regular Serving:** ½ cup dried corn (50 g), and ½ cup dried peach salsa (40 g). Rehydrate with 1 cup cold water (236 ml).

**Large Serving:** ¾ cup corn (75 g), and ⅔ cup dried peach salsa (50 g). Rehydrate with 1¼ cup cold water (300 ml).

After adding water, wait at least 2 hours. Excellent with a packet of tuna or chicken mixed in.

# 10. Fruits & Desserts

## Baked Pumpkin-Spice Apples

You're going to love the results of this apple-dehydrating project—hot pumpkin-spice apples that you can heat up on the trail or serve a la mode at home.

**INGREDIENTS:**

4 lb. apples (1.8 kg)
¼ cup fresh lemon juice
Lemon peel, grated
2 Tbsp. sugar, divided
2 tsp. ground cinnamon
½ tsp. ground ginger
½ tsp. ground nutmeg
¼ tsp. ground cloves

Yield: 8 servings of ½ cup each (25 g)

*Pumpkin spices include ground cinnamon, ginger, nutmeg, and cloves.*

### Baking & Dehydrating Spiced Apples

**Step 1:** Cut apples into quarters and remove cores. Slice quartered apples crosswise about ¼-inch thick. The extra thickness keeps the apples from getting mushy in the oven. Leaving the skins on also helps keep the apples intact as they cook.

**Step 2:** Place apples in deep baking dish and stir in the grated peel of 1 large or 2 small lemons, plus the lemon juice. Desired quantity is ¼ cup fresh lemon juice (60 ml).

Coat apples with pumpkin spices: 2 tsp. cinnamon, ½ tsp. ginger, ½ tsp. nutmeg, ¼ tsp. ground cloves, and 1 Tbsp. sugar.

**Step 3:** Cover baking dish with foil. Bake apples in preheated oven at 350°F (180°C) for 1 hour. At 30 minutes, stir apples to exchange the bottom apples with the top apples.

**Step 4:** As soon as the baked apples are cool enough to handle, place pieces in single layers, directly on mesh sheets of dehydrator trays. While placing apple slices on the trays, put any small or mushy pieces in a separate bowl. You want to set aside enough soft apples and juices to make 1 tray of apple leather.

**Step 5:** Hand mash all juices, soft pieces, and 1 tablespoon of sugar so that you end up with 1 cup sweetened pumpkin-spice apple slurry. Spread apple slurry thinly on dehydrator tray covered with nonstick sheet.

**Step 6:** Begin dehydrating apples and leather at 145°F (63°C) for the first 2 hours, then reduce temperature to 135°F (57°C) for the remaining time.

Total estimated drying time is 10–12 hours.

The 4 pounds of sliced apples will take up 3 Excalibur Dehydrator trays, and the mashed apple slurry will take up 1 tray.

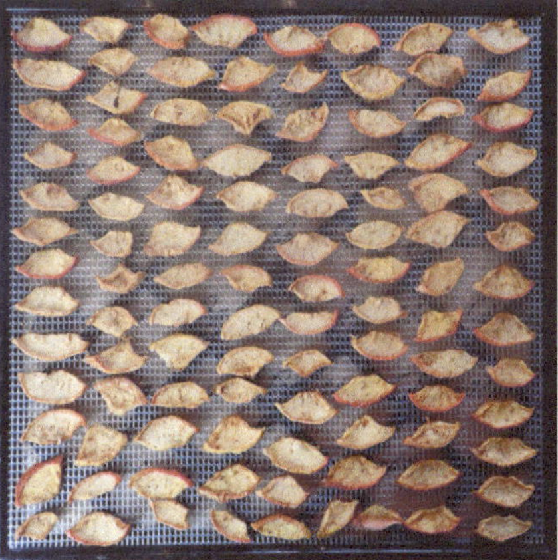

*(Left) Mashed apple slurry on Excalibur Dehydrator tray covered with nonstick sheet; (middle) folding dried apple slurry up in baking paper to keep from sticking to itself in storage, (right) dried pumpkin-spice apples.*

## Rehydrating Pumpkin-Spice Apples

*(Left) ½ cup dried apple slices (25 g), (middle) pieces of dried apple leather (7 g), (right) apple slices and apple leather rehydrated with ½ cup hot water (118 ml).*

Place ½ cup dried apple pieces (25 g) plus a few torn pieces of apple leather (7 g) in a pot with ½ cup water. Heat to desired temperature, allowing at least 20 minutes for apples to rehydrate. You can also rehydrate by adding hot water to the ingredients in a thermos food jar.

### At-Home Serving Suggestion:

Heat and rehydrate apples and leather pieces as describe above, and serve a la mode.

*Pumpkin-spice apples a la mode. Highly recommended!*

# Grated Apples with Lemon Juice

Dried grated apples are wonderful for snacking. They juice up in your mouth faster than dried apple pieces, and the lemon treatment imparts a nice citrus flavor. *They can also be used in **Bircher Muesli** on page 9.*

## Dehydrating Grated Apples

Peel and core apples, then grate them coarsely into a bowl of fresh-squeezed lemon juice. Stir as you go. Use 1 lemon per 5 apples grated. Although lemon juice helps to keep exposed apple flesh from turning brown due to oxidation, there will still be some light browning of the grated apples. They will still taste delicious.

*Dried grated apples.*

Spread grated apples and all juices on dehydrator trays covered with nonstick sheets. An Excalibur Dehydrator tray will hold 3 grated apples.

Dehydrate at 135°F (57°C) for 12–14 hours. Dried grated apples will be slightly pliable.

## Rehydrate Dried Grated Apples as a Filling for Tortilla Fruit Tarts

# Tortilla Fruit Tarts

Tortillas have long been the peanut butter–laden vessel of choice for backpackers. Flexible and ready to eat, tortillas make a convenient tart crust—no rolling pin required.

These tarts are filled with fruit, plus any extras you want to fold into them. Try spreading some peanut butter inside of one with grated apples.

If you hanker for a truly amazing treat, pack some foil and matches.

## How to Make Tortilla Fruit Tarts

To make small tarts, use taco-sized tortillas. To make big tarts, use burrito-sized tortillas. A small tart fits neatly in one hand. Go ahead and make one for your right hand—and one for your left.

Pack ¼ cup dried fruit for each small tart or ½ cup dried fruit for each large tart. Include a pinch or 2 of complementary items like nuts or chocolate. Try bananas with pecans, strawberries with sliced almonds and chocolate spread, and apples with walnuts.

Place dried fruit in a pot with an equal amount of water, apply heat, and rehydrate the fruit for about 10 minutes. You don't need to boil the fruit, but piping hot is nice.

Spoon the rehydrated fruit and any extra ingredients onto one side of a tortilla, and then fold the tortilla in half. Don't include any extra juices that remain after rehydration, as that will make the tortilla soggy.

Crimp the edges of the tortilla with a fork or spork, then flip it over, and crimp again from the other side. The seal will hold fairly well, but it may separate just a bit. Your crimping skills will improve with practice. Worst-case scenario, you end up with a tasty fruit taco.

Eat your tart with no additional heating, but if you have a campfire or grill with embers remaining after dinner, glaze and roast the tart to perfection in under a minute.

**Add a Sweet Glaze:** To make a glaze, moisten the top of the tart with a dribble of water remaining from rehydration, sprinkle a pinch of sugar and cinnamon over it, and rub it in.

**A Quick Roast:** Wrap the tart in 2 layers of foil. Don't put the foil-wrapped tart directly on the embers or it will burn quickly, and the tortilla will stick to the foil. Keep the glazed side up to avoid scorching. If you don't apply a glaze, flip the tart over a few times to get a light-brown toasting of both sides.

# Peach-Perfect Trail Treats

This section covers how to dehydrate peaches by slicing or grating them. It then shows how to make Peach Granola Clusters, Hot Peach Crumble dessert, or Peach Crunch Breakfast—all from the same bag of Peach-Perfect Trail Mix.

## Dehydrating Peaches

Peel the skins off with a sharp peeler, or leave the skins on. With squat-shaped clingstone peaches, cut the peaches into 4 chunks along the pit, and then slice the chunks thinly, about ⅛ inch.

Arrange peaches in a single layer directly on dehydrator mesh sheets.

Dehydrate at 135°F (57°C) for 10–12 hours.

Dried peaches will be pliable. Tear a few in half to check that no moisture beads up inside.

## Dehydrating Grated Peach Leather

Peaches can be reduced to a smoothielike consistency in a blender, or they can be grated for more texture. Grating produces a mash of juice and peach shreds.

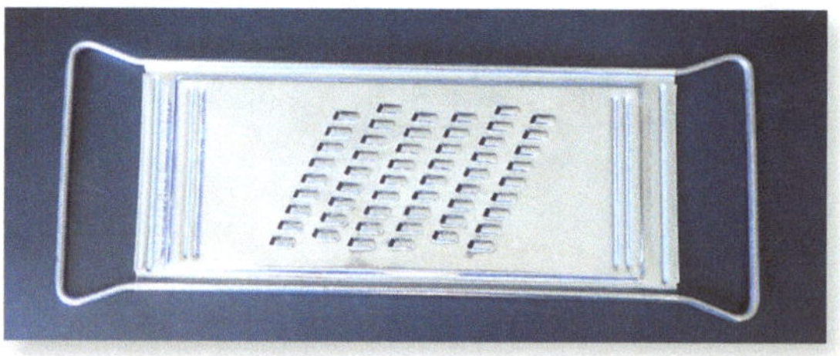

**PEACH LEATHER INGREDIENTS (PER TRAY):**

1 cup grated peaches
½ tsp. lemon juice
½ tsp. sugar

Spread grated or blended peaches thinly on dehydrator trays. For clingstone peaches, 4 to 5 peaches will reduce to 1 cup after blending/grating, which is a good quantity to spread on 1 tray.

Dehydrate at 135°F (57°C) for 10–12 hours. When peach leather is almost dry, flip it over, peel off the nonstick sheet, and finish drying directly on the mesh sheet.

## Peach Granola Clusters

Mix together 2 cups of granola (200 g) with 1 cup freshly grated peaches, including juices (225 g). Add 1 teaspoon each of lemon juice and sugar. Use your favorite granola mix, which can include nuts and seeds. Allow a few minutes for the granola to become fully saturated with the peach juices.

If using an Excalibur Dehydrator, this quantity fits on 1 tray covered with a nonstick sheet.

Dehydrate at 135°F (57°C) for 10–12 hours. After 8 hours, slide the nonstick sheet out from under the sheet of peaches and granola and continue drying directly on the mesh sheet. It should stick together. If you can't slide out the nonstick sheet, you can flip the tray over, and peel away the nonstick sheet.

Once dry, the granola-peach mix will easily break into clusters of varying sizes. The taste is wonderful—like fruity oatmeal cookies.

## Peach-Perfect Trail Mix

**INGREDIENTS:**

- 1 cup Peach Granola Clusters (80 g)
- ½ cup dried peaches (20 g)
- ½ cup grated peach leather (20 g)

Bag these items together for a high-energy, nutritious trail mix. Take your time eating this, if you can, to allow the juicy peach flavor to delight your taste buds.

*(Top to bottom): Grated peaches wet, grated peaches dry, granola clusters wet, and granola clusters dry.*

Hot Peach Crumble.

## Hot Peach Crumble

If your Peach-Perfect Trail Mix survives the day, turn it into Hot Peach Crumble for dessert.

Using the same ingredients and quantities as Peach-Perfect Trail Mix, place food in pot with 1½ cups of water (355 ml). Soak 5 minutes, and then heat until bubbling. Let sit for about 10 minutes with lid on pot. You will be amazed.

Peach Crunch Breakfast with milk.

## Peach Crunch Breakfast

This delicious, fast-energy no-cook breakfast is made with the same ingredients as Peach-Perfect Trail Mix, plus powdered milk.

**INGREDIENTS:**

1 cup Peach Granola Clusters (80 g)
½ cup peach leather (20 g)
½ cup dried peaches (20 g)
4–5 Tbsp. powdered milk
1½ cups cold water (355 ml)

Pack granola clusters and powdered milk separately from dried peaches and peach leather.

Combine dried peaches and peach leather in pot or bowl with 1½ cups of cold water. Let soak 10 to 15 minutes. Stir in powdered milk and continue stirring a minute to dissolve the peach leather. Add crumbled Peach Granola Clusters. Enjoy. Your day is off to a great start.

Peachy Fruit Cocktail with dried peaches, bananas and apples.

## Peachy Fruit Cocktail

Combine 1 cup mixed dried fruits (40–50 g) with 1 cup cold water (237 ml). Wait 30 minutes or longer for fruit to rehydrate. It gets better the longer you wait. If you would like to have some fruity juice to drink with the rehydrated fruit, use 2 cups of cold water (473 ml).

A thermos food jar is ideal for rehydrating fruit cocktail. Add cold water to the dried fruit after lunch to enjoy a refreshing treat later in the afternoon when it's hot.

# Watermelon Treats

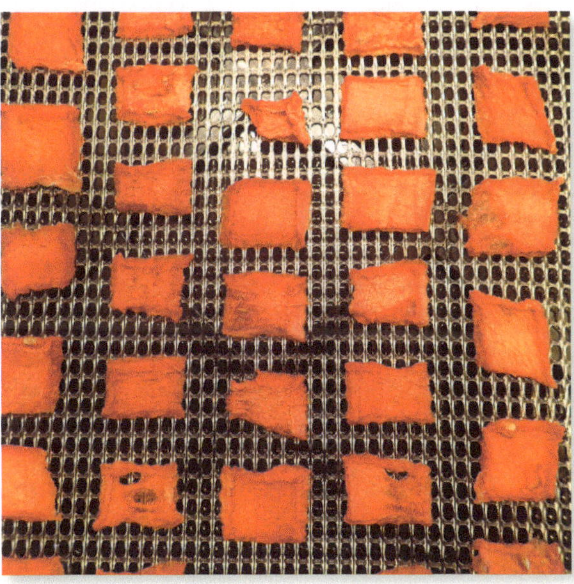

## Dehydrating Watermelon

Cut the watermelon crosswise into slices about an inch thick. If you cut an initial slice off the bottom, that will help you make even cuts by keeping the watermelon from rolling around. Remove seeds, and cut the rind away from the flesh.

Make ¼-inch-thick cuts all the way across each watermelon slice. Rotate ¼ turn after you make the ¼-inch cuts, and then make wider cuts, about 1 inch.

Place pieces directly on mesh dehydrator sheets. Place a nonstick sheet in the bottom of the dehydrator to catch any drips.

Drying watermelon on nonstick sheets is not recommended. The watermelon may turn gooey.

Dehydrate at 135°F (57°C) for 12–14 hours.

It does not hurt to dehydrate watermelon at 145°F (63°C). This will shorten the drying time by 1 or 2 hours.

The photos show that watermelon shrinks a lot when dried. The sugar in the fruit condenses, giving it that intense candy flavor.

Watermelon dries a little sticky. Store it at home in an airtight container. If it sits out, it will quickly absorb moisture from the air. For the trail, pack it in a Ziploc bag, rather than vacuum sealing it. The pressure of vacuum sealing will cause it to stick together.

Dried watermelon does not rehydrate well—it turns slimy. It's best to enjoy it dry.

Dehydrate cantaloupe in the same manner as watermelon.

# Banana Pudding

One way to dehydrate bananas is to blend them to a smoothielike consistency and spread them thinly (⅛-inch thick) on trays covered with nonstick sheets. If using an Excalibur Dehydrator, 1 cup of blended fruit is the perfect amount to spread on 1 tray to ensure even drying.

Bananas, when blended with no other fruits, may dry snappy—more like bark than pliable leather. Snappy banana bark is still very tasty. Another option is to blend bananas with other fruits or berries. Strawberries go great with bananas, as do pineapples.

## Banana-Pineapple Fruit Leather

**SERVINGS: 2**

**INGREDIENTS:**

2 large bananas (250 g)

2 thick slices pineapple (250 g)

Cut fruit into pieces, and blend until smooth. Spread thinly on dehydrator trays covered with nonstick sheets. If using an Excalibur Dehydrator, spread 1 cup per tray.

Dehydrate at 135°F (57°C) for 8–10 hours. When fruit leather is mostly dry with no wet spots, flip the leather over and peel away the nonstick sheet. Continue drying directly on mesh sheets until dry but still leathery.

**Yield:** 2 servings of ¾ cup leather each (46 g).

Enjoy banana fruit leather as is, or turn it into healthy fruit pudding with hot or cold water.

## Packing Fruit Leather

To pack fruit leather, so it doesn't stick to itself, fold it up in baking paper. Strawberry leather shown above.

Several individually wrapped fruit leathers can be vacuum sealed together, or just 1 could be vacuum sealed with the daily food rations. On the trail, the baking paper comes in handy as a placemat for preparing meal.

*Banana-Pineapple Pudding.*

## Banana-Pineapple Pudding

**SERVINGS: 1**

¾ cup Banana-Pineapple Leather (46 g)
1 cup cold water (237 ml)

Combine fruit leather and cold water. Stir until fruit leather is completely dissolved. Ready in minutes. It has a consistency like applesauce.

*Banana Split Pudding.*

## Banana Split Pudding

**SERVINGS: 1**

¾ cup Banana-Pineapple Leather (46 g)
Chocolate pieces (10 g) + extra goodies
1 cup cold water (237 ml)

**Extra goodies:** Add dried pineapple or strawberry pieces. A pinch of shredded coconut or almond slices wouldn't hurt.

Combine fruit leather, plus any dried fruit pieces, with cold water. Stir until fruit leather is completely dissolved. Ready in minutes. Garnish with chocolate pieces, coconut, nuts, etc.

*Banana Pudding with Chocolate & Nuts.*

## Banana Pudding with Chocolate & Nuts

**SERVINGS: 1**

½ cup dried banana slices (50 g)
Chocolate pieces (15 g)
Pecan or walnut pieces (15 g)
½ cup water (118 ml)

Gently heat dried banana slices in ½ cup water. Stir to desired pudding consistency. Dried banana slices disintegrate in minutes in hot water. Top with chocolate and nut pieces.

# Blueberries, Raspberries, and Strawberries

Dried berries are only fair for snacking, but they are a nice addition to oatmeal, cold cereal, and fruit cocktails.

*Berries before drying: raspberries (top), blueberries (middle), strawberries (bottom).*

## Dehydrating Berries

Dehydrate berries at 135°F (57°C) directly on mesh sheets.

Strawberries dry fast, in approximately 8 hours. Raspberries and blueberries usually take 12 hours or longer.

Raspberries are the most difficult of the berries to dry. Cut them into quarters or eighths with a sharp knife. They mush up a bit in the dehydrator and resist drying. Each berry is made up of around 100 drupelets, each one protecting a seed. You may feel like you have more seeds than fruit when done.

Blueberries dry best when cut into halves or quarters. Otherwise, the skin prevents the inside of the blueberries from drying completely.

Strawberries shrink the most when dried, so cut them into pieces ¼-inch thick.

## How to Make Berry and Fruit Powders

1. Make fruit leather by blending and dehydrating berries or fruits.
2. Tear fruit leather into pieces and place in blender. Grind into powder—about 1 minute.

**Good for Powdering:** Strawberries, blueberries, peaches, mangos. Shown above.

**Not Good for Powdering (Too Sticky):** bananas, apples, pineapples.

Add berry and fruit powder to smoothies, fruit cocktails, cold cereal, oatmeal, applesauce, and puddings.

# Blueberry-Apple Fruit Leather and Pudding

Although you don't need a thermos food jar to make fruit pudding from fruit leather, a thermos allows you to prepare it in advance. Rehydrate it with cold water for a juicy afternoon trail snack, or rehydrate it with hot water for the evening dessert.

**INGREDIENTS:**

4 apples
1 cup blueberries
1 Tbsp. brown sugar
¼ tsp. cinnamon
¼ cup apple juice

## How to Make Blueberry-Apple Leather

Combine apple chunks, blueberries, apple juice, sugar, and cinnamon in a pot, and bring to a boil. Frozen wild blueberries were used in this example. Reduce heat to low, and simmer for 20 minutes. Let cool, and blend until smooth.

Spread thinly on dehydrator trays covered with nonstick sheets. If using an Excalibur Dehydrator, 1 cup of sauce is perfect for 1 tray. This recipe took up 2 trays.

Dehydrate at 135°F (57°C) for 8–10 hours. Flip leather over after it is substantially dried, and peel off the nonstick sheets. Finish drying directly on mesh sheets.

**Yield:** ¾ cup dried leather per tray (46 g each), which makes a total of 2 servings.

Enjoy leather as is, or…

For a single serving of fruit pudding, combine ¾ cup fruit leather (46 g) with ¾ cup hot or cold water (177 ml). In hot water, it will reconstitute almost immediately. It takes 15 minutes of soaking and a little vigorous stirring to reconstitute with cold water.

To make juice, double the water. Let soak 15 minutes, combined with shaking in a container such as a thermos food jar.

Very refreshing on the trail.

# Sweet Potato Pudding

Sweet potato pudding is easy to make on the trail by rehydrating sweet potato bark or powder.

## How to Make Sweet Potato Bark with Baked Sweet Potatoes

More nutrients are retained by baking compared to boiling. Bake sweet potatoes on a baking pan for 50 minutes at 375°F (190°C). Use parchment paper under the potatoes to save yourself some scrubbing. After the potatoes have cooled, put 1 pound of chunked potatoes (453 g) into a blender with ½ cup apple juice, 1 tablespoon of maple syrup, and 1 teaspoon of cinnamon. Blend until smooth.

A pound of cooked sweet potatoes yields 2 cups blended mixture (473 ml). If using an Excalibur Dehydrator, 1 cup is the ideal quantity to spread thinly on each tray.

Dehydrate at 135°F (57°C) for 10–12 hours.

For efficiency, double or triple the recipe to use as many trays as possible.

Dried sweet potato bark makes a chewy trail snack that's loaded with nutrients. It reverts back into sweet potatoes with the addition of hot water. While not necessary, you can powder the dried bark by running it through a blender. Powdering reduces volume and slightly speeds up rehydration, but you lose the option of eating the bark as a chewy snack.

*1 cup of wet blended sweet potatoes yields ¾ cup bark or ⅓ cup powder. Weight of either bark or powder is 65 grams.*

## Making Sweet Potato Pudding

**SERVINGS: 1**

¾ cup bark, or ⅓ cup powder (65g)
1½ cups water (355ml)

Combine ¾ cup bark, or ⅓ cup powder, with 1½ cups water. Gently heat while stirring continuously until pudding is hot. It will thicken within 2 minutes. Another way to prepare it is to pour boiled water over the bark or powder in a separate container.

For the ultimate trail dessert, top the pudding with glazed pecan sauce.

## Glazed Pecan Sauce Topping

**SERVINGS: 1**

1 tsp. cornstarch
2 tsp. sugar
¼ cup pecan pieces
½ cup cool water

Combine cornstarch and sugar with ½ cup cool water. Stir until cornstarch dissolves. Do not add cornstarch to hot water because it will form clumps. Add ¼ cup pecan pieces, and light stove. Bring mixture to a light boil, and let it bubble for a minute. It will thicken and turn a nice shade of brown.

**Logistics:** Prepare the pudding first, and set aside in an insulated serving container. Then make the sauce and pour it over the pudding.

# 11. Drying & Packing Tips

## Food Drying Tips

**Tray Rotation:** Since the fan and heating element inside a dehydrator are in fixed locations, the air and heat flow may dry food on trays in some locations faster than others: top, middle, or bottom; left or right; and front or back. With square or rectangular dehydrators, rotating trays a quarter-turn or half-turn every few hours, as well as changing the position of trays from top to bottom, will even out and speed up drying. Rotating trays top to bottom is also helpful with round dehydrators.

**Rearrange the Food:** When a whole meal like chili or stew is substantially dry, pull the meal apart and redistribute it on the trays to expose more parts of the meal to airflow. Likewise, pull apart and redistribute rice, grated potatoes, and any food that sticks together.

**Dry Extra Vegetables:** When vegetables are cooked in a stew, they lose some of their color and texture. Include vegetables in the stew when you cook and dry it, but dry extra vegetables separately, and add them to the dried meal when you pack it for the trail. Steaming carrots for 6 minutes before drying them turns them dark orange, whereas carrots dried raw turn pale. Broccoli, green beans, peas, and corn also hold their colors better if steamed before drying.

**Cut Food Uniformly and Not Too Big:** You don't have to be precise when cutting fruits and vegetables, but if the pieces of food are similar in size, they will finish drying at the same time. After several hours of drying, tear any larger pieces of food in half. Fruit will dry faster, without risk of hidden moisture, if cut no more than a ¼-inch thick (½ cm). For foods you might dry in cubes, like baked sweet potatoes or butternut squash, shoot for cubes about ⅜ to ½-inch thick (1 cm).

**Don't Overload Trays:** Spread food on dehydrator trays in a single layer. Too much food on trays will greatly increase the drying time. Spread blended foods like sauces as thinly as possible. For Excalibur Dehydrator trays, which have the highest capacity per tray compared to other dehydrators, 1 cup, or a little more, of blended food is the ideal quantity to spread on nonstick sheets. For meals like chili or stew, you can dry up to 2 cups on an Excalibur Dehydrator tray. As the food dries and shrinks, stir it around a few times.

**Make Soup Thicker:** If your soup has a lot of broth, remove some of the soup solids and run them through a blender. Then add them back to the soup. Cooked potatoes are especially useful for thickening soups.

**Invest in Nonstick Sheets:** Although expensive on the front end, nonstick dehydrator sheets last for years, and it's much easier to spread blended foods on them than on single-use parchment paper. Foods like mashed potatoes, soups, and fruit purees will stay flat on nonstick sheets, but with parchment paper, they may draw up the paper as they dry. Once blended foods are dry, or almost dry, they can be easily removed from nonstick sheets, whereas food may not let go of parchment paper as well.

**Flip & Peel:** When blended foods like sweet potato bark, fruit leather, and tomato sauce are almost dry on nonstick sheets, flip them upside down and peel off the nonstick sheets. With the nonstick sheets removed, the increased airflow over the bottom side of the bark or leather will speed up drying.

**Fruit Leather Packing:** Fruit leather sticks to itself, especially when vacuum sealed. To avoid the difficulty of trying to pull it apart on the trail, fold up a single sheet of fruit leather in parchment paper.

# Home Storage Tips

Glass jars are convenient for storing dried foods until you are ready to assemble meals for a trip. They are more economical than disposable vacuum-seal bags, and there's no plastic waste. For short-term storage of a month or two, there won't be much negative impact on dried food if stored in jars without oxygen absorbers. For longer term storage in jars, use oxygen absorbers.

## Using Oxygen Absorbers

*(Left to right) 100 oxygen absorbers as they arrived in a sealed bag, dried olives and peas in small jars, and oxygen absorbers stored in a jar after the package was opened.*

Oxygen absorbers do a fine job of gobbling up oxygen, and they only cost a few pennies each. With oxygen absorbers, you can reuse jelly, sauce, and pickle jars. Clean and dry the jars and lids thoroughly before repurposing them for dried food storage.

Use the smallest jar that will hold the dried food. There will be less oxygen to remove if the jar is filled all the way.

Use a 50cc absorber for half-pint jars, 100cc for pint jars, and 300cc for quart jars. You may want to use the 100cc size oxygen absorbers for all jars; use 2 or 3 of them for large jars.

Once you open a package of oxygen absorbers, take out what you need for immediate use, and transfer the rest to a glass jar.

Exposure to light impacts the quality of dried food over time. Store jars in a dark place. A chest of drawers blocks light and makes accessing the jars easy. Label the lid of the jar with the name of the food and the date dried.

Oxygen-absorber suppliers usually sell Mylar bags, which can be used together with oxygen absorbers. You don't need a vacuum sealer if you pack meals in Mylar bags. One advantage of using Mylar bags with oxygen absorbers is that the bags don't scrunch up around the sharp edges of dried food, which sometimes causes vacuum-sealed bags to fail.

If you're already invested in a vacuum sealer and want to continue using it, there's another way to reduce the problem of bag punctures: Enclose an oxygen absorber and hit the seal button of the vacuum sealer before the bag gets to the scrunching stage. The oxygen absorber will remove the remaining oxygen. However, you'll never really know for sure if the vacuum bag has lost its seal or not, since maintaining the scrunch is evidence of a good seal.

# Vacuum-Sealing Tips

Vacuum sealing dehydrated meals for backpacking trips keeps food organized in the pack while protecting it from oxygen, moisture, and mice. Food odors are sealed inside the bag.

Some seals may fail when vacuum sealing if the sharp edges of dried ingredients puncture the bags.

To reduce the problem of vacuum-seal bags losing their seals, wrap each packaged meal in a paper towel before vacuum sealing. The paper towel acts like a cushion, and you'll find plenty of uses for the paper towel in camp. A second tip is to double seal each end of the vacuum bags.

## How to Vacuum Seal Dehydrated Meals

Begin by packing meals in sturdy plastic bags. Quart-sized freezer bags are a good size for packing large meals, and the bags have thicker plastic compared to flimsy sandwich-sized bags. Before you fill the bags, write the name of the recipe, the amount of water needed for cooking, and the date packed on the outside of each bag.

Place a little strip of paper across the zip closures to create a path for air to get sucked out of the bag during vacuum sealing.

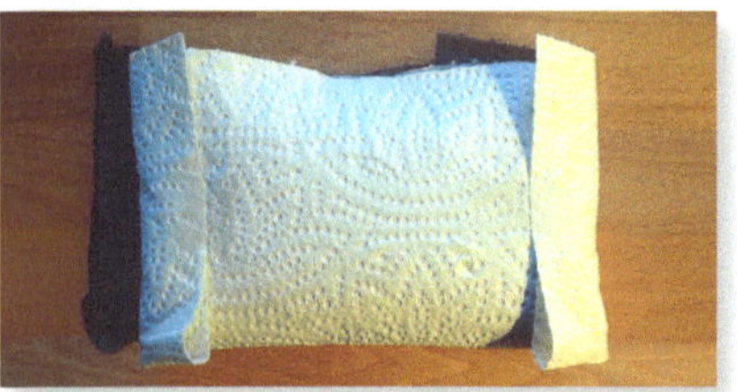

Place each filled bag on top of a paper towel. Flatten out the ingredients to fill the bag completely and evenly. By positioning any bags of powdered ingredients across the top, with no food above or below, you won't create any bulges.

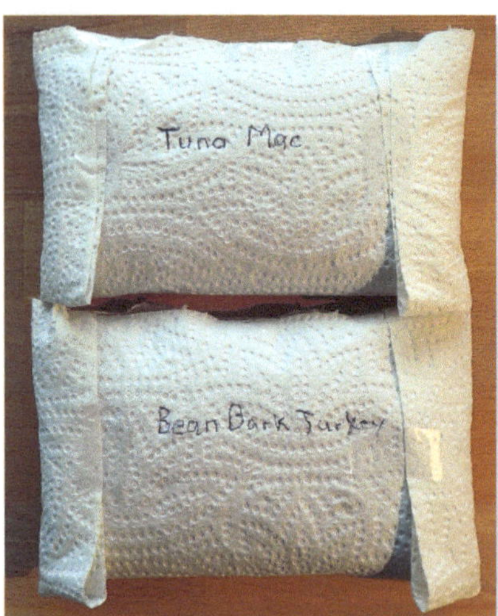


Fold bag and paper towel in half. Then, pull up sides of paper towel, and apply tape to attach. Apply 3 more pieces of tape to the longer open side. Write the name of each meal on the outside of the paper towel.

Two meals fit nicely in an 8-inch wide vacuum-seal bag, cut to 11 inches in length.

Buy 8-inch-wide rolls, and save money compared to buying individual bags.

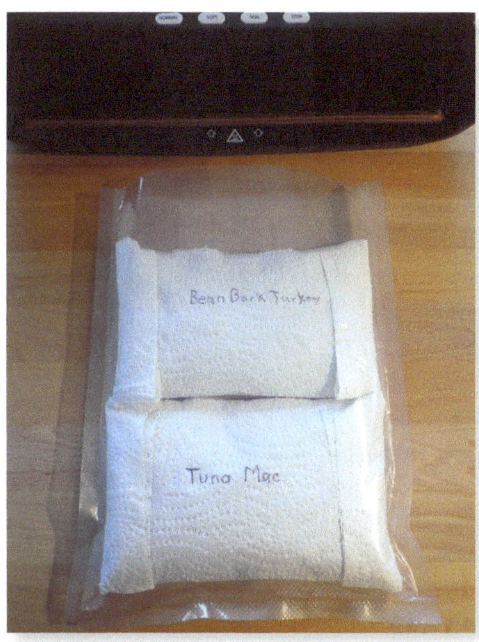


## Vacuum-Sealing Steps

Cut each bag to length (11 inches long is usually sufficient for 2 meals).

Seal one end. Double-seal to improve results.

Insert meals.

Seal other end.

Write the date on the bag, so you know to use it before other meals dried later.

This method of preserving complete meals is also ideal for home storage. If an emergency strikes, and you have to leave your home, you won't have time to fiddle around with assembling meals from a stash of dried ingredients stored in jars. Be ready to go with a supply of ready-to-eat meals.

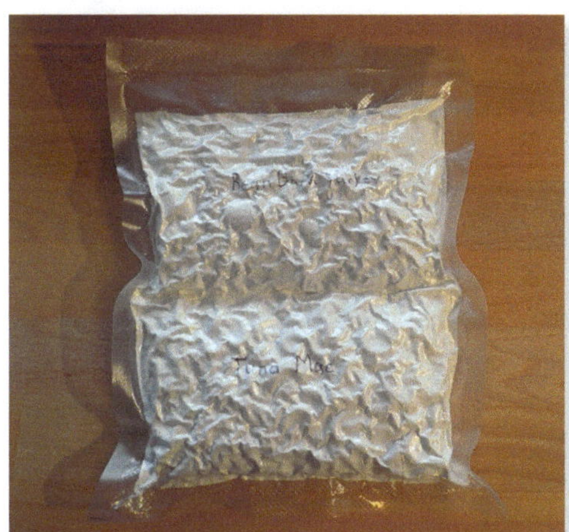

*If shopping for a vacuum sealer, go with one that has a built-in sliding bag cutter, as shown above.*

*A 31-day supply of vacuum-sealed meals.*

# Keep in Touch

## Subscribe to Trail Bytes

If you are not yet a subscriber, please visit **BackpackingChef.com** to sign up for *Trail Bytes.* See what's new on the website, and feel free to leave comments or ask questions.

Thank you for purchasing *Recipes for Adventure II: The Best of Trail Bytes*. Dominique and I trust you will enjoy the meals as much as we do. Having completed this collection of backpacking recipes from 100 issues of *Trail Bytes*, we're now cooking up ideas for the next 100 newsletters.

We wish you many exciting adventures in the kitchen and on the trail.

Chef Glenn & Dominique

**Notes:**

Happy Trails!

www.ingramcontent.com/pod-product-compliance
Lightning Source LLC
LaVergne TN
LVHW070126110826
845147LV00002B/198

* 9 7 8 1 7 3 7 4 6 3 0 0 9 *